Victory
in Jesus

Victory in Jesus

A Feast from Joshua

P. G. Mathew

GRACE & GLORY MINISTRIES
Davis, California

ISBN: 978-0-9771149-1-7
Library of Congress Control Number: 2006938885

Printed and bound in India by
Authentic India, P.O. Box 2190, Secunderabad 500 003
E-mail:printing@ombooks.org

Contents

About the Author vii

Foreword ix

Preface xi

1. Success in Life Guaranteed 1
   Joshua 1:1–9

2. Covenant Living 15
   Joshua 1:10–18

3. The God of Prostitutes 25
   Joshua 2

4. Problem Solved 37
   Joshua 3 and 4

5. Captain of the Lord's Army 49
   Joshua 5

6. Faith Is the Victory That Overcomes the World . . . 55
   Joshua 6

7. Sin in the Church 65
   Joshua 7

8. The Constitutional Convention of Canaan 73
   Joshua 8

CONTENTS

9. When We Don't Pray 83
   Joshua 9

10. When God Laughs, Watch Out! 97
    Joshua 10–12

11. The Faith of Caleb 109
    Joshua 14

12. Escaping the Death Penalty 117
    Joshua 20

13. The Joy of Christian Stewardship 125
    Joshua 21

14. The Faithfulness of the Covenant Lord 135
    Joshua 23

15. I and My Family Will Serve the Lord 145
    Joshua 24

Conclusion 159

Bibliography 161

Subject Index .163

About the Author

P. G. Mathew, a chemist originally from Kerala, India, holds three graduate degrees from Central and Westminster theological seminaries (USA). He is a former professor of Greek and systematic theology, and has traveled widely for Christian mission interests. He is the founder and senior minister of Grace Valley Christian Center in California; founder and president of Grace Valley Christian Academy; author of *The Normal Church Life: An Exposition of the First Epistle of John*; and the host of "Grace and Glory" radio program.

Foreword

I first heard P. G. Mathew preach about fifteen years ago. I was not a Christian then and I did not think it was possible for anyone to really know for sure that God exists, let alone to know God personally. So his words angered me; he spoke as though he knew God, and he made it clear that it was not just his opinion, it was the truth. His uncompromising preaching shook me out of my complacent agnosticism and launched me on a personal quest to find the truth, which ended about a year later when I committed my life to Christ.

Since that time I have had the blessing of having Pastor Mathew as my pastor. He is not just a biblical scholar, although he is that; he is also a devout man of God. He never fails to preach the word of God with clarity, power, love for people, and without fear of man. His life is a great model of a holy Christian life; he loves God and others, and possesses an unyielding commitment to the truth. Because I know Pastor Mathew well, I can recommend this book to you with great enthusiasm.

The scholar in Pastor Mathew helps the reader understand the language, history, and systematic theology of the book of Joshua; the pastor in him lovingly but firmly points out how that understanding should affect the way we live. His treatment of Joshua is a lucid presentation of the grand themes of the book and a compassionate guide to help us apply those themes to our own lives.

In the book of Joshua we see the unchanging God of love, power, judgment, and mercy in covenant relationship with man the creature. We behold the grace and blessings of God given to those who repent; the stern judgment and wrath of God poured out on those who refuse to repent; the victory God grants to those who go out and fight the battles he wants them to fight; man's sinful tendency to lean on his own understanding rather than seek the Lord; and the absolute need for the redeeming blood of Jesus Christ to cleanse us from our sins.

While guiding us through Joshua, Pastor Mathew inspires us with the great promises, faithfulness, and love of our covenant God. He confronts us with our sin and challenges us to repent of it, forsake it, and obediently follow Christ. He does what a good biblical scholar and pastor should do; he helps us understand and apply the word of God so that we can lead lives that are pleasing to God. He does not add to or subtract from the word but, by carefully exegeting the text, he lifts us up so that we can see reality more clearly.

The richest of fare awaits you. So take out your Bible, find a comfortable chair, a quiet place to read, and embark on a journey through Joshua. If you meditate on the word of God using this book as a guide, I promise that you will be richly rewarded. May God bless your reading!

RICHARD SPENCER, PhD
Davis, California
November 2006

Richard Spencer is a Professor of Electrical and Computer Engineering at the University of California, Davis, California.

Preface

The book of Joshua is the divinely
inspired historical account of God's leading the Israelites
to conquer and possess the promised land of Canaan.
Five hundred years earlier, the Lord had commanded
Abraham, "Leave your country, your people and your
father's household and go to the land I will show you"
(Gen. 12:1). He led Abraham to Canaan and made a
covenant with him, promising that, although his
descendants would be enslaved in another country
for four hundred years, one day they would return and
possess the land (Gen. 15). The Lord repeated this promise
to Abraham's son Isaac (Gen. 26:2–4) and then to Isaac's
son Jacob (Gen. 28:10–15).

The patriarchs never lost sight of God's covenant
promise. At the end of his life, Jacob spoke to his son
Joseph in Egypt: "I am about to die, but God will be
with you and take you back to the land of your fathers"
(Gen. 48:21). In turn, Joseph reassured his brothers, "I am
about to die. But God will surely come to your aid and
take you up out of this land to the land he promised on
oath to Abraham, Isaac and Jacob" (Gen. 50:24).

Through God's powerful deeds, Moses brought Israel
out of Egypt through the Red Sea into the wilderness.
God made a covenant with his people on Mount Sinai
and Israel promised to obey their covenant Lord of grace.
Yet they rebelled against the Lord and were killed.

But God's purpose to bring his people to Canaan could not be frustrated. He would fulfill his covenant with Abraham through Joshua son of Nun. As the commander of the army of the Lord, the angel of the Lord with his drawn sword defeated the Amorites through his servant Joshua and gave his people the rest of Canaan.

But the rest Joshua gave proved to be temporary. Israel became wicked and God threw them out to Assyria and Babylon. The rest Joshua gave was pointing to a greater rest—the rest of victory over sin, death, the devil, and the world.

The author of Hebrews declares that Joshua son of Nun did not give the Israelites the rest of forgiveness of sins and liberation from the fear of death. So God sent us another deliverer, Joshua the son of Mary, God-man, Jesus Christ, the sinless One who, through his perfect life and death on the cross, defeated the devil and canceled the penalty and power of sin.

This Jesus has given us everlasting rest and has made us triumphant over all our enemies in his triumph:

> He forgave us all our sins, having canceled the written code, with its regulations, that was against us and that stood opposed to us; he took it away, nailing it to the cross. And having disarmed the powers and authorities, he made a public spectacle of them, triumphing over them by the cross (Col. 2:13b–15).

> But thanks be to God, who always leads us in triumphal procession in Christ and through us spreads everywhere the fragrance of the knowledge of him (2 Cor. 2:14).

> "Where, O death, is your victory? Where, O death, is your sting?" The sting of death is sin, and the power of sin is the law. But thanks be to God! He gives us the victory through our Lord Jesus Christ (1 Cor. 15:55–57).

> Come to me, all you who are weary and burdened, and I will give you rest (Matt. 11:28).

Satan our enemy is still moving about like a roaring lion seeking to swallow us up. But by faith in the victory of Christ, we resist the devil and he flees from us. Thus we enjoy victory daily. The victory of Jesus is ours. He truly leads us in triumph always.

So "be strong in the Lord and in his mighty power. Put on the full armor of God" (Eph. 6:10–11) and overcome the devil daily by the blood of the Lamb and the word of our testimony (Rev. 12:11). In Jesus we are all overcomers. Victory in Jesus forever!

I wish to thank the members of Grace Valley Christian Center in California, where these sermons were first preached between January and May 2005. I would like to thank my wife Gladys, as well as Mr. Marc Roby, Dr. Lisa Case, Mr. Gregory Perry, Mrs. Sally Lischeske, and my personal secretary, Mrs. Margaret Killeen, for their help in preparing the manuscript for publication. Soli Deo Gloria!

P. G. MATHEW

1

Success in Life Guaranteed

Joshua 1:1–9

No one will be able to stand up against you all the days of your life. As I was with Moses, so I will be with you; I will never leave you nor forsake you.

Joshua 1:5

In the first chapter of Joshua we find an essential message for every Christian: God guarantees success to his people! What God promises, he performs, and what he starts, he will finish. Just as Joshua needed this assurance as he faced very real challenges in his time (ca. 1400 BC), so we too need God-given confidence as we confront the dilemmas and difficulties of our lives today.

"Moses My Servant Is Dead"

In what context was God's guarantee of success made to the Israelites? Mighty Moses had just died at 120 years of age. He was called "my servant" by the Lord (v. 2).

There is no greater honor for a human being than to be called "servant of God." But there is no servant who is without sin, except *the* Servant, Jesus Christ. Moses had disobeyed God (Num. 20:1–13), and God will not tolerate such conduct. Therefore, when Moses asked the Lord to permit him to lead the Israelites into Canaan, God said no. Moses was the last of that generation to die in the wilderness.

As a consequence, when the people were ready to cross the Jordan River and enter the promised land, they no longer had Moses to lead them. But God was not dead! God is eternal, immortal, immutable, and faithful. He cannot die; the mighty work of salvation that he began in Genesis will continue to advance unto its full fruition. God's will cannot be confounded; he always works according to his own eternal plan. No man is indispensable; when Moses died, God had a Joshua to continue the work.

Thirty-eight years earlier, God had chosen Joshua and prepared him for this very day. The Lord ordained him for service by filling him with the Holy Spirit. He appointed him as Moses' assistant so that he could learn how to lead God's people. Joshua was the general in charge when they fought against the Amalekites (Exod. 17:8–16). He was chosen to be one of the spies to enter Canaan, and he brought back a good report (Num. 13).

Now the Lord was directing Joshua to rise up, lead this nation of two million people across the overflowing river into Canaan, and conquer the land. But Joshua was tempted to be afraid, timid, weak at heart. How could he perform such a mighty task? We may also ask the same question as we face troubles and difficulties. How can we live a successful life and overcome our problems? God answered Joshua's concerns in a threefold manner: he guaranteed success, he mandated fidelity to his written word, and he promised to be present with his people.

God's Guarantee

In verse 2 God said to Joshua, "Now then, you and all these people, get ready to cross the Jordan River into the land I am about to give to them." Inherent in this command was God's promise of success. In other words, God was saying, "The time has come. There is no more delay. I am about to give this land to you, and you must believe in this promise."

God's promise of success is amplified in verse 3: "I will give you every place where you set your foot, as I promised Moses." Here the phrase "your foot" is plural, meaning not just Joshua's feet, but the feet of all the people of God. Note that passivity is ruled out; the people must set their feet in the land. They must believe God, obey him, and fight the battles necessary to appropriate his blessings. Yes, God gives victory, but we must also fight!

Verse 4 describes the extent of the territory God promised to Joshua. It was bounded by the Mediterranean Sea on the west, the River Euphrates on the east, Lebanon on the north, and the wilderness on the south. This large area is precisely what had been promised to Abraham in Genesis 15:18: "On that day the LORD made a covenant with Abram and said, 'To your descendants I give this land, from the river of Egypt to the great river, the Euphrates— the land of the Kenites, Kenizzites, Kadmonites, Hittites, Perizzites, Rephaites, Amorites, Canaanites, Girgashites and Jebusites.'"

God next declared to Joshua, "No one will be able to stand up against you all the days of your life" (v. 5). Every Christian must believe this promise and live by it. If we are servants of God, no one will be able to defeat us. No one! That is a promise we can rely on. The Lord went on to say, "As I was with Moses, so I will be with you." Man is powerless; he is nothing. But with God, we can do all things. The question we should ask is whether God is with us. If God is with us, success is assured. The verse concludes, "I will never leave you nor forsake you." In the Hebrew the meaning is, "I will never let you sink; I will never drop you or abandon you." As we face new challenges and trials, and perhaps even death itself, we must believe this promise of God.

The apostle Paul experienced the truth of this mighty affirmation when he was a prisoner of Rome. In 2 Timothy 4:10 he writes that Demas abandoned him, and that everyone in Asia forsook him. Then he states, "At my first defense, no one came to my support" (v. 16). Read on, however: "But the Lord stood at my side and gave me strength" (v. 17). We cannot ultimately rely on any human being. We need not worry, though, for our Lord will never let us sink, and he will never leave us nor forsake us. The eternal God is our refuge, and underneath are his everlasting arms. He will sustain us to the end.

In Joshua 1:6 we find another promise: "You will lead these people to inherit the land." That is an indicative statement with no contingency: "*You* will"—not anyone else. God had chosen Joshua many years ago for this task. God had trained him, ordained him, and filled him with wisdom and the Holy Spirit. Now he gave him this promise: "You will lead these two million people across this turbulent, overflowing river. You will conquer the land and divide it up as an inheritance for my people, fulfilling what I promised on oath to Abraham."

Whose promises are these? They are the words of the Lord, the Creator of the heavens and the earth. He spoke and the universe sprang into existence out of nothing. These are the words of the Lord who upholds the universe by the word of his power. These are the words of the Lord who governs all the affairs of history. These are the words of the Lord who made a covenant with Abraham five hundred years earlier, that he would have descendants, and that through him would come a

Savior in whom all the families of the earth would be blessed. These are the promises of the infinite, personal, covenant Lord who cannot lie.

Joshua needed only to look at recent history to know that these promises of God would be fulfilled, for everything God promised Abraham had come to pass in due time. He appeared in the burning bush and told Moses, "I am the God of your father, the God of Abraham, the God of Isaac and the God of Jacob. . . . I have indeed seen the misery of my people in Egypt. I have heard them crying out because of their slave drivers, and I am concerned about their suffering. So I have come down to rescue them from the hand of the Egyptians and to bring them up out of that land into a good and spacious land, a land flowing with milk and honey" (Exod. 3:6–8). God delivered the Israelites from Egypt through mighty miracles—the ten plagues and the parting of the Red Sea—which Joshua himself witnessed. He provided the Israelites with daily water and manna for forty years. He guided them continually by his presence, gave them everything they needed, and led them to the promised land. If Joshua could trust the Lord, so can we.

God's Mandate

God's guarantee of success, however, contained a mandate: Joshua must be fully devoted to God's powerful written word. In verse 7 God said, "Be strong and very courageous. Be careful to obey all the law my servant Moses gave you." At that time, the canon of Scripture consisted of only five books—the Pentateuch. Today God's will is more fully revealed in the sixty-six books of the completed Bible. We must understand that this Bible is the result of the creative activity of God: "All Scripture is God-breathed" (2 Tim. 3:16). It is not a human work; it is

God's work, and God is its primary author. Thus Scripture alone is the ultimate authority for the Christian. In this regard we have three obligations.

1. WE ARE TO OBEY GOD'S WORD

God warned Joshua in verse 7, "Be careful to obey all the law." This warning calls to mind Moses' one act of careless disobedience to God's word, which resulted in his not being permitted to lead God's people into the promised land (Num. 20:1–13). Joshua had a copy of the law, which Moses had given him. God now warned him to rely not on his subjective feelings and ideas but on that objective, historical word of God. The Lord reiterated the importance of this mandate in the next verse: "Be careful to do everything written in it." It is not enough to be a Bible student or a theologian skilled in exegesis. If we know the word of God but do not practice it, we are sinning. It is better not to open the Bible at all than to read and understand it but not do what it says. Unless we obey the word of God, we will not be blessed. In fact, knowing God's word without keeping it results in greater judgment.

In Matthew 7:21 Jesus says, "Not everyone who says to me, 'Lord, Lord,' will enter the kingdom of heaven.'" He is not speaking about pagans who have no understanding, but about those who know the Bible and yet do not obey it. They expect to enter the kingdom of God, but Jesus Christ will tell them, "I never knew you. Away from me, you evildoers!" (v. 23). Many churches today have abandoned the pursuit of a holy, obedient life and have subscribed to antinomianism, subjectivism, and autonomy. But autonomy is not Christianity, so it does not result in blessing.

Obedience to God's word is the key to success, power, courage, and wisdom. In Matthew 7:24 Jesus concludes, "Therefore everyone who hears these words of mine and puts them into practice is like a wise man who built his house on the rock." Proverbs 28:1 says, "The righteous are as bold as a lion." The righteous are those who, knowing the will of God, do it. Such people are confident and bold; they move forward, not backward. The obedient set goals and achieve them. They are unafraid, for it is sin and the guilt of sin that makes us afraid.

Furthermore, we are to obey exactly. The Lord continued his warning to Joshua: "Do not turn from it to the right or to the left" (Josh. 1:7). God takes no pleasure in a person who deviates from his direction as revealed in his word. When we travel, we are very careful to follow the map so we can reach our destination. God's word is the road map for life. To arrive at blessing, fellowship with God, and eternal life, we must follow his map with great care. In Deuteronomy 12:32 the Lord says, "See that you do all I command you; do not add to it or take away from it." And in Deuteronomy 17:11 we read, "Act according to the law they teach you and the decisions they give you. Do not turn aside from what they tell you, to the right or to the left." We have no freedom to interpret away the meaning of the word of God. We may not add to it or subtract from it. We may not be selective in our obedience to God's word. It is the narrow way that leads to life and blessing, as Joshua 1:8 concludes: "*Then* you will be prosperous and successful" (italics added).

2. WE ARE TO STUDY GOD'S WORD

True Bible study means working hard to understand the meaning of Scripture so that we can do what it says. We must study daily, systematically, and comprehensively as we go through the entire Bible. Such study includes meditation: "Meditate on it day and night" (Josh. 1:8). In other words, we are to apply our minds to the Scripture, making deduction and application. The Scriptures were written for our encouragement, hope, and warning. The word of God is profitable to us if we meditate on it, and God has given us minds for that very purpose. Philippians 4:8 says, "Finally, brothers, whatever is true, whatever is noble, whatever is right, whatever is pure, whatever is lovely, whatever is admirable—if anything is excellent or praiseworthy—think about such things."

In Psalm 119 the psalmist declares,

> Oh, how I love your law! I meditate on it all day long. Your commands make me wiser than my enemies, for they are ever with me. I have more insight than all my teachers, for I meditate on your statutes. I have more understanding than the elders, for I obey your precepts. I have kept my feet from every evil path so that I might obey your word. I have not departed from your laws, for you yourself have taught me. How sweet are your words to my taste, sweeter than honey to my mouth! I gain understanding from your precepts; therefore I hate every wrong path. (vv. 97–104)

When we love the word of God and meditate on it, we will avoid sin. When I see someone sinning on a regular basis, I know that person has quit reading the Bible seriously. Psalm 1 says, "Blessed is the man who does not walk in the counsel of the wicked or stand in the way of sinners or sit in the seat of mockers. But his delight is in the law of the LORD, and on his law he meditates day and night. He is like a tree planted by streams of water, which yields its fruit in season and whose leaf does not wither. Whatever he does prospers" (vv. 1–3).

3. WE ARE TO SPEAK GOD'S WORD
Verse 8 says, "Do not let this Book of the Law depart from your mouth." Fathers, it is your job to speak the word of God to your children and to your family. Speak it, because it alone is light and it alone gives guidance. "Let the word of Christ dwell in you richly as you teach and admonish one another with all wisdom" (Col. 3:16).

Speak the word of God—not human philosophies, which have no light. Secular philosophers cannot guide us in life. Everlasting principles are found only in the Holy Scriptures. Joshua faithfully spoke to his family, and near the end of his life he declared with confidence, "As for me and my household, we will serve the LORD" (Josh. 24:15).

We must speak God's word not only to our families but also to others. As Joshua taught the whole nation of Israel, so we also must speak the word of God to all nations, opposing all heresies, lies, and human philosophies. We must declare boldly, "The Bible says . . ." "God says . . ." "It is written . . ." Rather than embracing modernity, we must embrace the everlasting word of God. Why do some churches no longer speak God's word? Because they have made a conscious decision not to preach anything that would offend people. Public schools teach evolution, and so when biblical creation is preached, many people object. Prevailing secular philosophy declares that man is good, so when sin and the fall of man are preached, many are indignant. Modern man rejects the notion that he needs a savior, so when redemption in Jesus Christ is preached, many take offense. Churches that are more concerned with pleasing people than obeying God will not preach about such things. But genuine Christians fearlessly declare the whole gospel of God.

God's Promise

The Lord concluded his message to Joshua with the promise of his divine presence: "Have I not commanded you? Be strong and courageous. Do not be terrified; do not be discouraged, for the LORD your God will be with you wherever you go" (v. 9). God himself is the supreme commander, and there can be no doubt about the outcome of his mission. What great encouragement for Joshua to know that God would be with him wherever he went!

Imagine yourself in Joshua's situation. Nearby is the vast Jordan River. There are no boats, but God wants you to go across now, during the flood stage. We would be tempted to sit around and say, "We'd better figure this out first. I think God said to go over there, but that doesn't mean we have to go right now. Let's think about building boats or a bridge or something." Our nature is to plan projects and programs. But Joshua was to trust in God, listen to his voice, and obey.

The Jordan River was not the only problem Joshua faced. There were also giants in the land—the powerful Amorites. Earlier, when Joshua went to Canaan with a detachment of spies, most of them came back saying, "Yes, it is a beautiful land that flows with milk and honey. But the cities are fortified, and there are giants there. In our own eyes we seemed as grasshoppers." When we don't truly believe that God is with us, such obstacles seem insurmountable. How could Joshua lead two million people across this great river and defeat their giant enemies? On his own, he could not. But Joshua had the promise of God's presence, and so do we.

Once, in anger at the stubbornness of his people in the desert, God had threatened, "I will not go with you" (Exod. 33:3). Moses was alarmed by such a prospect, so he prayed, "If your Presence does not go with us, do not send us up from here." The Lord, moved by Moses' plea, graciously replied, "My Presence will go with you, and I will give you rest" (Exod. 33:14–15). Rest means salvation, peace, inheritance, and joy. The Lord made the same promise to Joshua: "As I was with Moses, so I will be with you" (Josh. 1:5). That promise is still true for us today. As he was with Moses and Joshua, so God will be with you and me. Therefore we can face the future, our enemies, persecution, and death itself, without fear.

In the last chapter of the book of Matthew, Jesus tells us, "All authority in heaven and on earth has been given to me. Therefore go and make disciples of all nations, baptizing them in the name of the Father and of the Son and of the Holy Spirit, and teaching them to obey everything I have commanded you. And surely I am with you always, to the very end of the age" (Matt. 28:18–20). The Christian life is based on this reality of God's presence with us. The One who is Lord, the Creator of the ends of the earth and governor of the universe; the One who is the Lord of history, who defeated death itself by his death on the cross; the One who rose from the dead—this One says to us, "I will never leave you nor forsake you" (Josh. 1:5). He says, "In this world you will have trouble. But take heart! I have overcome the world" (John 16:33).

We must never forget that this God who promises to be with us is a warrior. He is the self-existing, self-sufficient, covenant Lord. He fights every battle for us and delivers us out of the hand of our enemies. So Moses said to Joshua as he prepared to enter the promised land, "Do not be afraid of them; the LORD your God himself will fight for you" (Deut. 3:22). Moses used this language also in Exodus 15:3: "The LORD is a warrior; the LORD is his name. Pharaoh's chariots and his army he has hurled into the sea." Moses did not take credit for all the miracles God had performed. He knew that God himself had fought the battle and silenced Pharaoh, who had challenged him by saying, "Who is the LORD, that I should obey him?" (Exod. 5:2).

Additionally, we must never forget that this Warrior God opposes *all* sin, including our own. If you are practicing sin as a Christian, you are doing so because you do not believe that God is with you. God's presence with his people is powerfully depicted in his coming to Mount Sinai in Exodus 19 and 20. The whole mountain smoked and quaked, there was thunder and lightning, and the people were told not to touch the mountain, for it was holy—God was there. The people trembled with fear and pleaded with Moses, "Speak to us yourself and we will listen. But do not have God speak to us or we will die" (Exod. 20:18–19). What often passes today for reverence is superficial when compared with this scene on Mount Sinai. It is true that Christians should worship God with joy; but when we really see God, we will also tremble in holy fear. Psalm 2:11 tells us, "Serve the LORD with fear and rejoice with trembling."

The realization of God's presence with us will inspire us to lead blameless lives. In Exodus 20:20 we read, "Moses said to the people, 'Do not be afraid. God has come to test you, so that the fear of God will be with you to keep you from sinning.'" If we really believe that the eternal, infinite, almighty, all-holy, all-just God is with us, our entire outlook will change. Our thinking will be different, our speech will be different, our work lives will be different, and our marriages will be different. All our behavior will change for the better, because we will be living to please this most holy God who is with us.

God's Promises Fulfilled

People of God, be strong and courageous. Do not be terrified or discouraged—God is with us! Believe his promises. Trust in his unchanging, eternal word. Rest in his presence. Fear him and obey his commands. Move forward with him; our success is guaranteed. God has promised to save us, and all his promises will be fulfilled, even as we read in Joshua 21:43–45: "So the LORD gave Israel all the land he had sworn to give their forefathers, and they took possession of it and settled there. The LORD gave them rest on every side, just as he had sworn to their forefathers. Not one of their enemies withstood them; the LORD handed all their enemies over to them. Not one of all the LORD's good promises to the house of Israel failed; every one was fulfilled."

Not only so, but there is also One who is greater than Joshua, the Lord Jesus Christ, who in the fullness of time was born of a woman in order to fulfill every promise of God. By his life and death on the cross, he destroyed the devil once for all and freed us from death itself. He promises true rest to all who trust in him, and he calls the weary to himself, saying, "Come to me . . . I will give you rest" (Matt. 11:28). He gives an inheritance to us and brings us into his promised land of eternal salvation. In him we are blessed with every spiritual blessing in the heavenly places: "For no matter how many promises God has made, they are 'Yes' in Christ" (2 Cor. 1:20).

Be strong in the Lord, therefore, and fight your spiritual enemies, for Christ has already defeated them. Resist the devil, and he will flee from you. We are told that neither death nor life nor anything else in all creation is able to separate us from the love of God. We have the power of God's promise, the power of God's word, and the power of God's presence. Our Warrior Savior goes out to conquer, and none of his promises will fail. He always leads us in triumph, and finally he will present us before God's glorious presence without fault and with inexpressible joy. This is God's purpose, and he will achieve it.

What about you? Are you still wandering and restless? Is your life without meaning or purpose? Are you confused and lonely? Our greater Joshua, the Savior Jesus, is here. Cry out to him, and he will forgive your sins and clothe you with his righteousness. Jesus Christ died for our sins and was raised for our justification. Mark it down: from this day forward, he will make you successful and prosperous as you follow him.

2

Covenant Living

Joshua 1:10–18

> *You are to help your brothers until the Lord gives them
> rest, as he has done for you, and until they too have taken
> possession of the land that the Lord your God is giving
> them.*

Joshua 1:14–15

The first chapter of Joshua teaches us a
valuable lesson about covenant life. Today, individualism,
self-interest, and self-centeredness are exalted. We glory
in the philosophy that says, "I'll do what I want to do,
when and how I want to do it, and I don't care what anyone
else thinks." But the moment we become Christians, such
thinking must come to an end. As believers we are called to
live in covenant relationship with God and each other.

A covenant is an agreement between two or more
persons; therefore, covenant life is community life. A
covenant person will seek not his own interest but that
of the entire community. For example, when a man
marries, he enters into a covenant with his wife and
ceases to be a single person. He keeps the covenant of

marriage by self-denial and faithfulness to his marriage vows. In the same way, when a believer is baptized, he confesses Jesus Christ as Lord and enters into a covenant with him. From that point on, he no longer lives for himself but for Christ. Our greatest idol is self, but Jesus demands that we deny self, take up the cross daily, and follow him. Likewise, when a believer joins a local church, he enters into a covenant to seek the welfare of that community.

Many, however, who enter into a covenant-based life fail to live up to their promises and commitments. Instead of seeking the good of others, they end up pursuing their own interests and pleasures. They become self-seekers. The Bible rebukes such people, but praises those who keep their oaths even when it hurts (Ps. 15:4). Joshua was a person who kept his word. Take, for example, his agreement with the Gibeonites (Josh. 9). As inhabitants of Canaan, the Gibeonites were slated to be destroyed by the Israelites. But they deceived Joshua and the leaders into making a covenant of peace with them, and Joshua kept that covenant, even though the whole community grumbled against him (9:18).

The ultimate example of one who lived a true covenant life is our Lord Jesus Christ. He agreed to become incarnate, to live a perfect life under God's law, and to die a sacrificial death in behalf of the elect people of God. At Gethsemane Jesus prayed, "My Father, if it is possible, may this cup be taken from me. Yet not as I will, but as you will" (Matt. 26:39). His desire to do God's will was unwavering, despite the agony of the hour. And so, in keeping with God's will, Jesus went obediently to the cross. He kept covenant.

Jesus Christ calls us all to live such a covenant life, putting the interests of God and our fellow believers before our own. An excellent illustration of covenant life is found in the history of the tribes of Reuben, Gad, and the half-tribe of Manasseh, especially as recorded in Numbers 32, Joshua 1:10–18, and Joshua 22.

The Sin of Rejecting Covenant Life

After leaving Egypt, the Israelites wandered in the wilderness for forty years due to their own unbelief and rebellion. An entire generation murmured against the covenant the Lord had made with them; as a result, they died in the desert. They did not enter into their inheritance of rest in the promised land because of their disobedience.

Now the next generation was east of the Jordan River, ready to enter the land. They had already defeated Sihon king of Heshbon and Og king of Bashan (Deut. 1:4), and had thus gained possession of their territories on the east side of the Jordan River, stretching from the Arnon River in the south to Mount Hermon in the north, beyond the Sea of Galilee. The Israelites now controlled hundreds of Amorite cities, as well as the fertile lands of Bashan and Gilead.

Numbers 32:1 and Deuteronomy 3:19 tell us that the tribes of Reuben, Gad, and the half-tribe of Manasseh possessed large numbers of livestock. Seeing that the land east of the Jordan was suitable for grazing, they approached Moses and the other leaders with this request: "Please do not make us cross the Jordan, but let us possess these fertile lands on the east side of the Jordan." This request sprang from their sinful rejection of the covenant obligations of community life. They were rejecting God's plan and not living by faith. They were placing their own interests above those of all the other Israelite tribes. They were behaving like Lot did many centuries before. Genesis 13:10–11 tells us that "Lot looked up and saw that the whole plain of the Jordan was well watered, like the garden of the LORD, like the land of Egypt . . . So Lot chose for himself

17

the whole plain of the Jordan." Lot made his choice for one reason—he owned many cattle. Lot based his decision on sight, not on faith.

Jesus once warned his followers, "The pagans run after all these things" (Matt. 6:32). "These things" refers to money and material possessions. Pagans live for money and make decisions based on the possibility of making more money. They have no interest in the life of faith. If the employer says, "I'll give you a raise if you go to New York," they say, "No problem. I'll go to New York." If the employer says, "I'll give you lots of money if you work ninety-five hours a week," they reply, "No problem at all. I will do anything to make another buck." How many times have we made similar decisions! We promote our own interests above those of God and his community.

Moses was displeased when these tribes requested to remain in Transjordan territory, thus showing their unwillingness to cross the Jordan with their brothers and fight the Lord's battles with them. In anger he called them a "brood of sinners" (Num. 32:14) and asked, "Shall your countrymen go to war while you sit here?" (Num. 32:6).

Just as the tribes rejected community life in favor of a self-centered life, so do many believers today selfishly reject their covenant responsibilities. One example of forsaking one's covenant vows is divorce, which arises in most cases from sinful selfism. Similarly, when a believer removes himself from the life of a local church for selfish reasons, he is rejecting the covenant responsibility he assumed when he was received into membership.

Repentance and Renewal of the Covenant

Happily, we go on to read in Numbers 32:16–19 that these two and a half tribes repented of their sins and renewed their covenant. They entered into an agreement with Moses, Joshua, Eleazar, and the other leaders, which included three promises: first, their armed men would cross over the Jordan with their brothers; second, they would go ahead of everybody else as the vanguard to face the most dangerous fighting; and third, they would not return to their homes until every Israelite had received his inheritance.

Now, it is one thing to renew one's covenant promises; it is entirely another thing to keep those promises, especially when it hurts. When God makes a promise, we can rely on it, for God is not a man that he should lie, nor does he ever change his mind. He promised rest to all the tribes and he would keep that promise. But would the tribes of Reuben and Gad and the half-tribe of Manasseh fulfill what *they* had promised?

Moses was not convinced by their words, but he agreed to their covenant renewal conditionally. In fact, almost all promises in the Scripture are based on a condition. It must be stated here that it is by grace that we fulfill these conditions (Phil. 2:12, 13). We will not be saved until we repent and believe on the Lord Jesus Christ. We cannot receive God's blessings unless we first meet his conditions. Just so, in Numbers 32:20–21 we find several conditional "ifs" that Moses placed before these tribes: "If you will do this—if you will arm yourselves before the LORD for battle, and if all of you will go armed over the Jordan before the LORD until he has driven his enemies out before him. . . ."

What did Moses promise to the tribes if they fulfilled these conditions? The answer is found in verse 22: "Then when the land is subdued before the LORD, you may return . . . and this land will be your possession before the LORD." If these tribes fulfilled the conditions, *then* they could return to their land and be blessed. God blesses only those who walk in the way of obedience.

What about our own lives? How many promises have we made as Christians? We cried out to God with tears, in repentance and renewal, and we vowed many things—

only to forget the next morning what we promised! Think of the promises you made to the Lord at your baptism, to your church when you joined it, to your spouse at your marriage, to God and the church when you dedicated your children. Have you fulfilled them? We are to be like God our Father and keep our word, even when it hurts.

Keeping Covenant Promises

Joshua now reminded the two and a half tribes of their covenant responsibilities: "Remember the command that Moses the servant of the LORD gave you . . . all your fighting men, fully armed, must cross over ahead of your brothers. You are to help your brothers until the Lord gives them rest" (Josh. 1:13–15). In verse 16 we see the unconditional surrender in their reply: "Then they answered Joshua, 'Whatever you have commanded us we will do, and wherever you send us we will go.'" There was no limit to their pledge of obedience. Then they added, "Whoever rebels against your word and does not obey your words, whatever you may command them, will be put to death" (v. 18). In other words, they were telling Joshua, "Put us to death if we do not obey you!"

Having made this promise, the tribes went on to keep it. In Joshua 4 we read about the miraculous crossing of the Jordan: "Now the priests who carried the ark remained standing in the middle of the Jordan until everything the LORD had commanded Joshua was done by the people, just as Moses had directed Joshua. The people hurried over, and as soon as all of them had crossed, the ark of the LORD and the priests came to the other side while the people watched. The men of Reuben, Gad and the half-tribe of Manasseh crossed over, armed, in front of the Israelites, as Moses had directed them. About forty thousand armed for battle crossed over before the LORD to the plains of Jericho for war" (vv. 10–13). These covenant-keepers crossed over in front of the others, just as they had agreed to do. They went on to fight in every battle on the west side of the Jordan, helping achieve victory for Israel. In Joshua 12 we find a list of the thirty-one kings they helped defeat.

The tribes had also promised that they would not return home until all the Israelites had gained possession of their inheritance (Num. 32:18). In Joshua 21:43–45 we are told, "So the LORD gave Israel all the land he had sworn to give their forefathers, and they took possession of it and settled there. The LORD gave them rest on every side, just as he had sworn to their forefathers. Not one of their enemies withstood them; the LORD handed all their enemies over to them. Not one of all the LORD's good promises to the house of Israel failed; every one was fulfilled." The Israelites had received their inheritance, yet even still these valiant men remained in the land. As good soldiers, they were waiting for the general's order. So in Joshua 22:1 we read, "Then"—meaning after they fought and defeated all Israel's enemies—"Joshua summoned the Reubenites, the Gadites and the half-tribe of Manasseh and said to them, 'You have done all that Moses the servant of the LORD commanded, and you have obeyed me in everything I commanded.'" What a glorious statement!

Thus, these covenant people made promises and kept them. When confronted with their sins, they repented, saying, "We were selfish and we repent of it. We will go over the Jordan and fight every battle for the good of the whole community." They put their lives in danger for their brothers. Notice, they did not fight just for a day, or a month, or a year, but for seven long years. They paid a high price to keep their covenant. For seven years they were away from their wives, their children, and their possessions. Yet we do not read of even one time when these people murmured during their years of service to Israel. They trusted in God and kept their promises, obeying everything Moses and Joshua commanded.

The two and a half tribes had learned that covenant life is about commitment and relationship. So Joshua commended them, saying, "For a long time now, to this very day, you have not deserted your brothers" (22:3–4). As Christians we are not alone; we are brothers and sisters, joined together in the bond of Christ. A church is not a group of individuals who merely meet on Sundays to hear the word of God and then rush out the door when the service is over. As many members in one body, we are connected to one another, and we each have particular gifts to be used for the common good. We are our brothers' keepers.

Joshua finally told the faithful tribes, "Now that the Lord your God has given your brothers rest as he promised, return to your homes" (Josh. 22:4). Then Joshua gave them a very important exhortation. Although their military obligation was over, their covenant obligation to the Lord continued. Joshua told them, "But be very careful to keep the commandment and the law that Moses the servant of the Lord gave you: to love the Lord your God, to walk in all his ways, to obey his commands, to hold fast to him and to serve him with all your heart and all your soul" (22:5). Covenant life is an ongoing relationship with God and his people.

Blessings for Obedience

Joshua 22:6 says, "Then Joshua blessed them and sent them away, and they went to their homes." When we walk faithfully in covenant, we experience God's blessing; when we walk in disobedience, we experience his curse. The first generation of Israelites did not enter into rest because of their unbelief; they all died in the wilderness. But the next generation went home with Joshua's blessing. The conditions for God's blessing have not changed with time. There are people today who say, "In the Old Testament period, people had to obey God, but with the coming of the New Testament age, we do not have to." Not true! Jesus Christ says, "If you love me, you will obey what I command" (John 14:15). Our God does not change, nor does the nature of his covenant with his people.

Covenant obedience brought real, abiding blessing to the Israelites. This blessing, pronounced by Joshua, consisted in the Lord's bestowing on them great material and spiritual benefits. Thus, the blessing was not just empty words; it meant something! In verse 8 we read, "[Joshua] blessed them, saying, 'Return to your homes with your great wealth—with large herds of livestock, with silver, gold, bronze and iron, and a great quantity of clothing.'" Notice, they had come over the Jordan carrying only their weapons, but now they returned with great wealth. There is always blessing when we keep the covenant and walk in obedience.

Curses for Disobedience

Just as there is blessing when we keep God's covenant, so also there is a curse for failing to keep it. When these tribes originally promised fidelity to the covenant, Moses did not fully believe them. So he warned them, "If you fail to do this, you will be sinning against the LORD; and you may be sure your sin will find you out" (Num. 32:23). In other words, they would suffer consequences for breaking the covenant.

Self-seeking is a dangerous enterprise, especially for a Christian. A self-seeking person will not be blessed. The Bible gives many examples of self-centered people who rejected covenant life, and therefore received curses instead of blessings. Yet how many of us really believe that what we say matters? We make promises and enter into agreements readily. We say yes quickly, only to forget what we said a day or a week or a year later. And we think that no matter what we do, God's blessing will still come to us. But it will not. Our sin will find us out.

Application

In closing, let us consider six imperatives for covenant living:

First, we must make decisions based on spiritual rather than material considerations. We must not be like the pagans, running after the things of the world and rejecting covenantal obligations to pursue selfish interests.

Second, we must realize that true riches consist in relationships. Our relationship with the Lord, the relationship between a husband and wife, the relationship of parents and children, our relationship with our brothers and sisters—these are the true treasures of life.

Third, we must be convinced that our sin will find us out, and that every infraction of a covenant will be revealed in due time. We must take to heart the truth that God will not bless those who turn away from their covenant promises.

Fourth, we must keep our word even, and especially, when it hurts, knowing that if we do this, we will never be shaken (Ps. 15:5).

Fifth, we must make every effort to maintain the unity of the community of believers, established by the Holy Spirit. If we contribute to the disruption of the Lord's covenant community, he will judge us.

Sixth, we must love our brothers and sisters in the Lord. Jesus said, "A new command I give you: Love one another. As I have loved you, so you must love one another" (John 13:34). How did Jesus love us? By dying on the cross for our sins! Therefore, we too must lay down our lives for our brothers. This is serious community life. This is covenant living.

3

The God of Prostitutes

Joshua 2

Now then, please swear to me by the Lord that you will show kindness to my family, because I have shown kindness to you. Give me a sure sign that you will spare the lives of my father and mother, my brothers and sisters, and all who belong to them, and that you will save us from death.

Joshua 2:12–13

In Jesus' day, the Pharisees considered themselves alone to be righteous. They hated publicans and prostitutes, regarding them as sinners to be avoided at all costs. Such self-righteous people have no need of Jesus. But Jesus came as a friend of sinners. He came to seek and to save that which was lost. The truth is, according to God's word we are all publicans and prostitutes, for "all have sinned and fall short of the glory of God" (Rom. 3:23). Only in Jesus can we become truly righteous and children of the heavenly Father. Joshua 2 tells the story of God's love for wicked sinners as depicted in the salvation of Rahab the prostitute.

After the death of Moses, Joshua began preparations to lead the people of Israel into the promised land. In Joshua 2:1 we read, "Then Joshua son of Nun secretly sent two spies from Shittim. 'Go, look over the land,' he said, 'especially Jericho.' So they went and entered the house of a prostitute named Rahab and stayed there."

The Divine Purpose

Why did Joshua send these secret agents to Jericho? Surely it was not necessary to obtain new intelligence, for God had already revealed that the Canaanites would be afraid of the Israelites and that God would deliver the land over to his people (Exod. 15:15–16; Num. 14:8–9). In fact, the great wall of Jericho would soon fall without a fight under God's own power. Why, then, did Joshua send the spies? It was for a divine purpose: God had determined to save a notorious sinner, a leading prostitute of that wicked city, from destruction. The spies were God's messengers, sent to bring salvation to Rahab the harlot and her entire extended family.

When the people of Israel reached the border of Canaan, the iniquity of the Canaanites was full to overflowing, and the entire population was under the wrath of God (see Gen. 15:16; Deut. 9:4–5). Yet the first act of God in Canaan was not one of destruction, but of salvation—the salvation of a prostitute in Jericho. Rahab was one of God's elect, chosen from all eternity to be holy and blameless in his Son, Jesus Christ. In time, through Joshua's spies, she was effectually called and justified.

Rahab was not merely an innkeeper, although the Hebrew word used to describe her can have that meaning; she was also a prostitute, as we read in Hebrews 11:31 and James 2:25, where she is called *pornē*, prostitute. We should not sanitize her, as some would like to do. Rahab was an idol-worshiping Amorite woman who was as full of iniquity as all the other citizens of Jericho; thus, she deserved the same total destruction that they experienced—

they were killed by the sword, and the whole city was burned (Josh. 6:21–24). Instead of judgment, however, Rahab received the grace of God, as the Bible declares, "Where sin abounded, grace did much more abound" (Rom. 5:20 KJV).

In 1 Timothy 1:13–15 Paul speaks about God's attitude toward wicked sinners and the grace God shows to them: "Even though I was once a blasphemer and a persecutor and a violent man, I was shown mercy because I acted in ignorance and unbelief. The grace of our Lord was poured out on me abundantly, along with the faith and love that are in Christ Jesus. Here is a trustworthy saying that deserves full acceptance: Christ Jesus came into the world to save sinners—of whom I am the worst."

God, in his patience, had given the citizens of Jericho opportunity to repent and sue for peace. They knew that the God of Israel had powerfully delivered his people out of Egypt by drying up the Red Sea so that they could pass through on dry ground. They knew this God had recently destroyed the kingdoms of the Amorite kings Sihon and Og. They knew very well the power of the God of Israel. Yet most in Jericho opposed him and his people. They refused to repent and believe. They would rather fight than surrender and be saved.

Rahab's Steps of Faith

1. HEARING

Rahab did not join the people of Jericho in their enmity and unbelief toward the God of Israel. She had heard of the great redemptive acts of Israel's God from people who visited her brothel. It is amazing how God uses even sinners to declare the gospel, that his elect may be saved!

We cannot be saved unless someone is sent to proclaim the good news of redemption to us. We first have to hear the gospel, for faith comes by hearing. As Paul says in Romans 10:14, "How can they believe in the one of whom they have not heard?" Rahab heard the gospel, and when the spies came, she told them, "We have heard how the LORD dried up the water of the Red Sea for you when you came out of Egypt, and what you did to Sihon and Og, the two kings of the Amorites east of the Jordan, whom you completely destroyed. When we heard of it, our hearts melted and everyone's courage failed" (Josh. 2:10–11).

2. BELIEVING

Not only did Rahab hear, but she also believed. Hebrews 11:31 says of her, "By faith the harlot Rahab perished not with them that believed not, when she had received the spies with peace" (KJV). Many other citizens of Jericho had also heard the gospel, but they perished because they did not believe. Sadly, Israel too had been guilty of such unbelief in the past. Forty years earlier, Moses had sent out twelve spies to explore the land of Canaan (Num. 13). When they returned, ten of them influenced the entire assembly of Israelites with these words of unbelief: "We cannot defeat them. They are more powerful than we are." Imagine, the vast majority of Israel, God's chosen people, did not believe in his mighty power! Yet, when this Amorite prostitute heard about the Lord, she believed and said, "I know that the LORD has given this land to you and that a great fear of you has fallen on us, so that all who live in this country are melting in fear because of you" (2:9). May God help us to so believe his word, that we too may experience his saving power.

3. CONFESSING

After hearing and believing the accounts of God's mighty acts on behalf of the Israelites, Rahab confessed what every child of God must confess: "For the LORD your God is God in heaven above and on the earth below"

(v. 11). God expects his people to make such a declaration. In Deuteronomy 4:39 the Israelites were commanded to "acknowledge and take to heart this day that the LORD is God in heaven above and on the earth below." We find the same requirement in the New Testament: "If you confess with your mouth, 'Jesus is Lord,' and believe in your heart that God raised him from the dead, you will be saved" (Rom. 10:9). Out of the mouth of a prostitute, God brought the true confession that the God of Israel is the God of heaven and earth, the true and only God, and that all other gods are false.

4. PRAYING

Correct confession, however, is not sufficient to accomplish salvation. Anyone can make a correct profession of faith, but orthodoxy alone never saves anyone. After hearing, believing, and confessing the gospel, the sinner must take the final step—praying to God for salvation. Rahab did just that by pleading with his representatives, as recorded in verses 12 and 13: "Now then, please swear to me by the LORD that you will show kindness to my family, because I have shown kindness to you. Give me a sure sign that you will spare the lives of my father and mother, my brothers and sisters, and all who belong to them, and that you will save us from death."

5. REGENERATION

Sometime between hearing about God and being visited by the spies, Rahab must have experienced regeneration, the new birth produced in the heart by the Holy Spirit. Unless a person is born of God he cannot repent, believe, confess, and pray for salvation. The Holy Spirit had worked in Rahab's heart, and she was born again, so she was able to pray, "Save us from death." Her prayer was effectual, for Romans 10:13 gives us this promise: "Everyone who calls on the name of the

Lord will be saved." As Rahab called upon the name of the Lord, she was saved. She was saved temporally, from the present danger of the Israelite invasion. But of infinitely greater importance, she was saved eternally, from the wrath of God against sinners.

Faith That Works

We know that Rahab had saving faith because she demonstrated it by her deeds. James testifies under the inspiration of the Holy Spirit: "In the same way, was not even Rahab the prostitute considered righteous for what she did"—that is, by her works of faith—"when she gave lodging to the spies and sent them off in a different direction? As the body without the spirit is dead, so faith without deeds is dead" (James 2:25–26). If people say they believe in God, but do not evidence their faith by love for God and obedience to him, their faith is counterfeit.

Salvation is by grace alone through faith alone, but saving faith is not dead faith. Faith alone justifies, but faith that justifies is not alone at any time. True faith is faith that works. This is exactly what Paul says in Ephesians 2:10: "For we are God's workmanship, created in Christ Jesus to do good works, which God prepared in advance for us to do."

If someone claims to be a Christian but does not love God or keep his commandments, he is phony and his faith is empty. There is no difference between his faith and that of the devil (James 2:19). This is hard preaching for modern Christians to accept, because they want to be considered "true Christians" even though they refuse to obey God. Saving faith always produces good works. For example, husbands will love their wives, wives will submit to their husbands, and children will obey their parents immediately, exactly, and with joy.

It is such works as these, done in loving obedience to God's commands, that validate the Christian's claim to saving faith.

The Works of Rahab's Faith

Let us examine the faith of Rahab and the works it produced. When the spies came, Rahab welcomed them, hid them from the authorities, and sent them away to safety. These were dangerous actions on her part, for ancient laws such as the Code of Hammurabi dictated that any person who discovered an enemy spy must turn that spy over to the king or face execution. Rahab risked her life in protecting the Hebrew spies.

Rahab continued to work out her faith as she obeyed the three directives given her by the spies. First, she was to keep the Israelites' plans a secret (v. 14). Second, she must tie a scarlet cord in the window through which she had let the spies down (v. 18). Third, she must gather her family into her house and keep them inside until the army of Israel came (vv. 18–19). Being a prostitute, Rahab was not married and had no children. But we can deduce from this passage that she prayed not only for her own salvation but also for the salvation of her father, mother, brothers, sisters, and all the people who belonged to them. What a great faith!

Rahab faithfully kept the Israelites' secret. When the king's officials questioned her, she did not reveal the whereabouts of the spies. We may ask, "Didn't she lie, and isn't lying a sin?" There are differing opinions among Christians regarding the propriety of her actions. Some would say she should have told the truth. But it is also arguable that this was a war situation in which deception was necessary as a tactic of war. Since Rahab considered herself to be a believer in the God of Israel, Jericho and the people of Jericho were now her enemies.

In this situation she was not obligated to speak the truth to the king of Jericho.

When the spies left, Rahab immediately tied the scarlet cord in the window (v. 21). The scarlet cord hearkens back to Exodus 12, when the Hebrews were required to kill the Passover lamb and apply its blood on their doorposts and lintels so that the angel of death would pass over their houses. These are powerful symbols of the blood of Jesus Christ, which saves the sinner from the wrath of God. It is possible the cord was given to Rahab by the spies themselves. God not only saves, he also provides the means of salvation!

Finally, Rahab immediately went to all her relatives and said, "This land is given to the Israelites by their God, in whom I believe. Jericho is going to be destroyed immediately. But I have pleaded with this God, and he has agreed to save every one of you as long as you come to my place and stay there." What amazing mercy God showed to Rahab and her family! The Bible tells us they all came and were saved. In Joshua 6:22–23 we read, "Joshua said to the two men who had spied out the land, 'Go into the prostitute's house and bring her out and all who belong to her, in accordance with your oath to her.' So the young men who had done the spying went in and brought out Rahab, her father and mother and brothers and all who belonged to her. They brought out her entire family and put them in a place outside the camp of Israel."

Contrast the response of Rahab's family with that of Lot's in Genesis 19. An angel came from heaven to the city of Sodom and warned Lot, "God is going to wipe this place out and burn it because of its wickedness." But when Lot relayed this terrible news to his sons-in-law and urged them to flee with him, how did they respond? "No deal," they replied. "You are joking." They did not believe. Not only that, but Lot's own wife also did not believe, and as a result she became a pillar of salt (v. 26). But Rahab's family believed her warnings and laid hold of the refuge offered to them.

In Luke 16 we read about the rich man and Lazarus. The rich man was full of the good things of this world and did not begin to think about his salvation or that of his family until he died and was in hell. By then it was too late. His eternal destiny was fixed, and the day of salvation for him was past. Let me tell you, now is the accepted time, now is the day of salvation. Now is the day we must call upon the name of the Lord and be saved. Now is the time we must pray for our families, in faith, just as Rahab did.

Many of us have a hard time believing God will save our children, our parents, or our siblings. But let me assure you, God's covenant extends to you and to your family, even to your extended family. The promise is unto you and your children, from generation to generation (Acts 2:39). Even an aged person can come to faith in Christ before he passes away. We must never give up praying in faith for the salvation of our family members.

Exodus 12 speaks about this principle of whole-family salvation. In verses 1–3 we read, "The LORD said to Moses and Aaron in Egypt, 'This month is to be for you the first month, the first month of your year. Tell the whole community of Israel that on the tenth day of this month each man is to take a lamb *for his family*'" (italics added). We find the same idea in Joshua 24, when Joshua presented a choice to the Israelites, telling them, in essence, "If you want to worship idols, that's up to you. If you want to turn away from God, that's up to you. . . . But as for me and my household"—I am sure this included his servants as well—"we will serve the LORD" (v. 15). Likewise, in Acts 16, the Philippian jailer cried out, "What must I do to be saved?" And the answer came, "Believe in the Lord Jesus, and you will be saved—

you and your household" (vv. 30–31). These accounts are among many in Scripture demonstrating that God includes whole families in his plan of salvation.

From Prostitute to Princess

Rahab's story does not end in Joshua 2. She and all her family became citizens of Israel (Josh. 6:25), and she married a prince of the tribe of Judah by the name of Salmon (Matt. 1:5). When she was a prostitute in Jericho, Rahab had no husband or children. But God transformed her, causing her to become a true Israelite, desirable even to a prince in Israel! The Bible tells us Rahab became the mother of Boaz. In his old age, Boaz married another Gentile, Ruth the Moabitess, who, like Rahab, had turned from paganism to serve the living God. Ruth became the mother of Obed, who became the father of Jesse, who became the father of David, the ancestor of Jesus. Thus Rahab the prostitute became an ancestress of Jesus Christ, the Son of David, the Savior of the world.

The truth is, brothers and sisters, we were all Rahabs. We were dead in trespasses and sins, but God chose us in Christ to be made alive by the power of the Holy Spirit. We see this divine work elucidated in Titus 3:3–7:

> At one time we too were foolish, disobedient, deceived and enslaved by all kinds of passions and pleasures. We lived in malice and envy, being hated and hating one another. But when the kindness and love of God our Savior appeared, he saved us, not because of righteous things we had done, but because of his mercy. He saved us through the washing of rebirth and renewal by the Holy Spirit, whom he poured out on us generously through Jesus Christ our Savior, so that, having been justified by his grace, we might become heirs having the hope of eternal life.

Just as Rahab's story did not end with her deliverance from Jericho, so our story does not end with our justification. When God saves us, he saves us from our sins and he commands each of us, "Go now and leave your life of sin" (John 8:11). God raises us up with Christ and seats us with him in the heavenly realms, and he is changing us from glory to glory. We, like Rahab, are being transformed from prostitute to princess. We are his bride, whom he is making holy, blameless, and radiant. God loved us when we were prostitutes, but we do not remain prostitutes. He makes us princesses of great glory. Rahab married Salmon, the Israelite prince. But we are marrying Jesus Christ, the King of kings and the Lord of lords.

Revelation 19:5–8 proclaims this glorious truth:

> Then a voice came from the throne, saying: "Praise our God, all you his servants, you who fear him, both small and great!" Then I heard what sounded like a great multitude, like the roar of rushing waters and like loud peals of thunder, shouting: "Hallelujah! For our Lord God Almighty reigns. Let us rejoice and be glad and give him glory! For the wedding of the Lamb has come, and his bride has made herself ready. Fine linen, bright and clean, was given her to wear." (Fine linen stands for the righteous acts of the saints.)

What about You?

Have you heard the message of the cross—that Christ died for our sins and was raised for our justification? Have you believed that message and trusted in Jesus Christ, the only Savior, for your salvation? Have you confessed with your mouth "Jesus is Lord" and believed in your heart that God raised him from the dead? Like Rahab, have you called upon the name of the Lord to save you from the wrath of God about to be poured out upon sinners? If you have, then you can rejoice in the assurance that God has saved you.

What if you have not yet called upon God? Take heart—the promise of salvation still stands. Everyone who calls upon the name of the Lord will be saved. If God can save a prostitute like Rahab, he can save you. God saves only sinners, so we must acknowledge that we have sinned. I urge you to call out to him, "Have mercy upon me, a sinner," that he may save you and your family today.

4

Problem Solved

Joshua 3 and 4

The priests who carried the ark of the covenant of the Lord stood firm on dry ground in the middle of the Jordan, while all Israel passed by until the whole nation had completed the crossing on dry ground.

Joshua 3:17

As God's people journey together toward his Celestial City, they will face new situations and difficulties along the way. We may face unemployment, relocation, family problems, sickness, surgery, or even imminent death. We will face the devil, who goes about like a roaring lion, desiring to swallow us if possible. We will wrestle "against the rulers, against the authorities, against the powers of this dark world and against the spiritual forces of evil in the heavenly realms" (Eph. 6:12).

These hard realities of life can be likened to the Jordan River that Joshua and the Israelites needed to cross before they could enter the promised land. There is a Jordan for the people of God to cross, and we are told it is at flood stage. Who is competent for such a task? Only God can lead us successfully through life's insurmountable challenges, and he will. We have his promise and his presence to help us.

Believing God's Promise

Long ago, God swore to Abraham that his descendants would inherit the beautiful land of Canaan (Gen. 12:7). In due time, God appeared to Moses and promised to deliver his people out of Egypt and bring them into the promised land (Exod. 6:6–8). With his powerful, outstretched hand, God performed mighty miracles and delivered the Israelites from their Egyptian bondage. But the Israelites suffered from unbelief. When Moses sent spies to Canaan to scout out the land, the majority of them returned with a negative report:

> "We went into the land to which you sent us, and it does flow with milk and honey! . . . But the people who live there are powerful, and the cities are fortified and very large. . . . We can't attack those people; they are stronger than we are. . . . The land we explored devours those living in it. All the people we saw there are of great size. . . . We seemed like grasshoppers in our own eyes, and we looked the same to them." (Num. 13:27–28, 31–33)

Only two spies, Joshua and Caleb, gave a report consistent with God's word:

> "The land we passed through and explored is exceedingly good. If the Lord is pleased with us, he will lead us into that land, a land flowing with milk and honey, and will give it to us. Only do not rebel against the Lord. And do not be afraid of the people of the land, because we will swallow them up. Their protection is gone, but the Lord is with us. Do not be afraid of them." (Num. 14:7–9)

The people of Israel, when presented with these two divergent views, chose to believe the majority report. They saw only the problems, not God. Because they refused to believe God's promise, they failed to cross the Jordan and enter into Canaan's rest. That generation died in the wilderness.

Now, some forty years later, the faithful Lord of the covenant was ready to guide the children of the disobedient generation across the overflowing Jordan into the promised land. Like their fathers, they also sent out spies, but these men brought back a positive report. They related to Joshua what Rahab had told them: "We have heard how the Lord dried up the water of the Red Sea for you when you came out of Egypt, and what you did to Sihon and Og, the two kings of the Amorites east of the Jordan, whom you completely destroyed. When we heard of it, our hearts melted and everyone's courage failed" (Josh. 2:10–11). The spies drew the proper conclusion, one that agreed with God's earlier promise: "The LORD has surely given the whole land into our hands; all the people are melting in fear because of us" (2:24). After so many years in the desert, this generation of Israelites believed God, and they were ready to cross the Jordan.

The spies' report encouraged Joshua. But more than that, God himself encouraged Joshua, telling him what he would do at this new time, in this new situation, with this new generation: "Now then, you and all these people, get ready to cross the Jordan River into the land I am about to give to them—to the Israelites. I will give you every place where you set your foot, as I promised Moses. . . . As I was with Moses, so I will be with you; I will never leave you or forsake you. . . . Be strong and courageous. Do not be terrified; do not be discouraged, for the LORD your God will be with you wherever you go" (1:2–5, 9). God wanted his people to cross the Jordan and enter Canaan, and with his help, every one of them would do so.

Crossing an overflowing river was not what the people would have chosen for themselves. But when we walk with the Lord, we do not have to worry about the unforeseen difficulties we will face. We can have confidence that they are appointed by God, and that he wants to take us through them to make us spiritually strong. The way may be new to us, but it is not new to God, and we can be assured that God, who has been faithful to us in the past, will be faithful to us in the future.

The Necessity of Consecration

Before the Lord would lead his people into Canaan, they had to prepare themselves. Therefore Joshua told the people, "Consecrate yourselves, for tomorrow the LORD will do amazing things among you" (Josh. 3:5). To experience this kind of supernatural help, God's people must be holy. They must be united, disciplined, organized, under authority, and wholeheartedly obedient to the divine word.

We cannot follow a holy God unless we also are holy, both internally and externally. God himself commanded, "Be holy, because I am holy" (Lev. 11:44). The people had to wash their clothes, wash themselves, reaffirm their loyalty to the covenant, get rid of all idols, and repent of their sins. Most importantly, they had to believe, for no one could enter Canaan without faith in the covenant Lord. In the same way, we too experience God's power only when we fully consecrate ourselves to him. We cannot expect divine deliverance if we are practicing sin.

God Does Amazing Things

Joshua told the Israelites, "Tomorrow the Lord will do amazing things among you." Joshua's optimism was based on God's promise. Our God is a God of wonders. He is

"I AM THAT I AM," the eternal, personal, Creator, Redeemer God. He is God Almighty, El-Shaddai. He is the Warrior-Savior, who always leads his believing people in triumph, solving their problems in remarkable ways. This God, who accomplished deliverance for his people by sending mighty plagues against the Egyptians, would surely do amazing things again.

Joshua encouraged the people, saying, "Come here and listen to the words of the LORD your God. This is how you will know that the living God is among you and that he will certainly drive out before you the Canaanites, Hittites, Hivites, Perizzites, Girgashites, Amorites and Jebusites. . . . As soon as the priests who carry the ark of the LORD—the Lord of all the earth—set foot in the Jordan, its waters flowing downstream will be cut off and stand up in a heap" (Josh. 3:9–10, 13).

Notice, Joshua first said, "Come here and listen to the words of the LORD your God." God's word reveals a God who does amazing things, and to whom our problems are never amazing. Our troubles seem great to us only if we fail to see the greatness of our God. Whatever our predicament, the answer to it lies in hearing and believing the word of God. That is why we must come to the word frequently, listening intently when it is preached. When we see the power of God in his word, we will be strong and courageous in the face of all our problems.

Joshua then said, "You will know that the living God is among you." Idols are the works of human minds and hands; they have no life and cannot save us. But our God is the living and true God. He is with us, and he will help us cross the Jordan.

Finally, Joshua related the specifics of God's promised deliverance—the crossing of the Jordan River and the conquest of Canaan. The people believed God's word and acted accordingly; thus, they experienced his miraculous intervention: "As soon as the priests who carried the ark reached the Jordan and their feet touched the water's edge, the water from upstream stopped flowing. . . . So the people crossed over" (Josh. 3:15–16). God's promise to us has always been, "Believe my word and you shall be saved." The first generation refused to believe God's word, and they perished in the wilderness. But the second generation believed, and they crossed the Jordan into the promised land. God solved their problems.

Seeing God's Presence

Not only did the Israelites have God's promise, they also had his very presence with them, for God met with them above the ark of the Testimony (Exod. 25:22; Num. 7:89). This ark was the most sacred object in the tabernacle, Israel's place of worship. A rectangular wooden box, forty-five inches long, twenty-seven inches wide, and twenty-seven inches high, it was covered in gold inside and out. Upon its lid of solid gold stood two golden cherubim facing each other, with wings that stretched upward and met in the center. Inside, under the wings of the cherubim, were the two tablets of the law, the Ten Commandments, which expressed the holy character of God. Poles were inserted through rings attached to each side of the ark so it could be carried by the priests.

The ark symbolized God going in front of his people to deal with their enemies. In Numbers 10:33–35 we read about the Israelites' journey in the wilderness: "So they set out from the mountain of the LORD and traveled for three days. The ark of the covenant of the LORD went before them during those three days to find them a place to rest. . . . Whenever the ark set out, Moses said, 'Rise up, O LORD! May your enemies be scattered; may your foes flee before you.'"

Whenever the Israelites saw the ark, they knew that the invisible God was with them to guide them, fight for them, and save them. In Joshua 3, the Lord confirmed this promise to Joshua, and gave him these words for the people: "When you see the ark of the covenant of the LORD . . . then you will know which way to go. . . . This is how you will know that the living God is among you. . . . The ark of the covenant of the Lord of all the earth will go into the Jordan ahead of you" (Josh. 3:3–4, 10–11). Joshua then instructed the priests, "Take up the ark of the covenant and pass on ahead of the people. . . . When you reach the edge of the Jordan's waters, go and stand in the river" (Josh. 3:6, 8). The people and the priests did exactly as they were commanded. What was the result? The waters of the Jordan were cut off before the ark of the covenant of the Lord, providing safe passage to the other side (Josh. 3:15–17). God is the way, and he makes the way for us. He goes ahead of us, and our job is very simple—we are to follow.

Problem Solved

Forty years earlier, God had miraculously parted the Red Sea in order to deliver his people from Egypt. He commanded Moses, "Raise your staff and stretch out your hand over the sea to divide the water" (Exod. 14:16). Moses did so, and all that night the Lord drove the sea back with a strong east wind and turned it into dry land. The Israelites passed through the sea with walls of water to their right and left (Exod. 14:21–22).

Now the Lord was about to part the water again, but in a different manner. This was a new place, a new time, and a new generation. Yet God remains the same. This time there was no staff and no wind, only this command with a promise: "Carry the ark and go into the water. When the soles of your feet touch the water, it shall be divided, and you will walk through on dry land." The priests carrying the ark believed this word from God and stepped into the river. When the soles of their feet touched the water, it divided. The upstream water rose up in a heap and the downstream water immediately emptied into the Dead Sea. After leading the people across the Jordan, Joshua, who forty years earlier had also witnessed the parting of the Red Sea, said, "The LORD your God did to the Jordan just what he had done to the Red Sea when he dried it up before us until we had crossed over. He did this so that all the peoples of the earth might know that the hand of the Lord is powerful and so that you might always fear the LORD your God" (Josh. 4:23–24).

Joshua 3:17 tells us, "The priests who carried the ark of the covenant of the LORD stood firm on dry ground in the middle of the Jordan, while all Israel passed by until the whole nation had completed the crossing on dry ground." We are told everyone crossed over to the western side— not one perished. When we consecrate ourselves to hear, believe, and obey the word of God, God does amazing things. He solves all our problems.

Build a Memorial

God then instructed Joshua to build a memorial commemorating this supernatural event. In Joshua 4:4–9 we read, "So Joshua called together the twelve men he had appointed from the Israelites, one from each tribe, and said to them, 'Go over before the ark of the Lord your God into the middle of the Jordan. Each of you is to take up a stone on his shoulder, according to the number of the tribes of the Israelites, to serve as a sign among you. . . . These stones are to be a memorial to the people of Israel forever.' . . . So the Israelites . . . took twelve stones from the middle of the Jordan . . . and they carried them over with them. . . . Joshua set up the twelve stones . . . and they are still there to this day."

What is the purpose of such a memorial?

1. IT IS A SIGN FOR THE PRESENT GENERATION

We are told that Joshua set up the twelve river stones at Gilgal, on the west bank of the Jordan River. They were to be a sign to the Israelites, a remembrance of what God had done for them there. Those who participated in the Jordan crossing were to benefit from this sign (4:6, 20). There are times when Christians, though they have crossed over the Jordan, become discouraged and fearful. We tend to forget God and his saving deeds. When this happens, we must look at such memorials in our own lives and believe that he who delivered us in the past will save us again.

2. IT IS A SIGN FOR FUTURE GENERATIONS

A memorial provokes questions. Joshua instructed the people, "In the future, when your children ask you, 'What do these stones mean?' tell them that the flow of the Jordan was cut off before the ark of the covenant of the Lord" (4:6–7). The stone memorial was to be a catalyst for conversation, providing opportunity for the Israelites to tell their children, "God did amazing things! God solved our biggest problem!"

The phrase *tell them* in the Hebrew is more accurately translated "cause them to know for certain." When our children ask questions, it gives us an opportunity to evangelize them. We must make sure they know, appreciate, and experience the salvation of the Lord. We do not want to give them mere intellectual knowledge; we want them to entrust themselves to this God who is among his people, this living God who does amazing things, this God who saves.

3. IT IS A SIGN FOR ALL PEOPLES ON EARTH

Joshua 4:24 says, "He did this so that all the peoples of the earth might know that the hand of the LORD is powerful." God's purpose is that in Abraham all the nations and families of the earth be blessed. This blessing comes through the knowledge of God, and this knowledge comes through hearing. The people of God are to tell all the people of the world about the wonders of God, so that they also may put their trust in him and be saved.

Our Memorial—the Bible

The stone memorials of Joshua's day have been lost to history, but God's deeds have been written down in a book. We must look in the pages of the Bible to discover the amazing things our God has done. When we come to church we must listen carefully to his word as it is preached, for it tells us about him and what he can do for us.

Our God still does amazing things—he saves us, making a way where there is none. As we are told in Zechariah 4:6, this mountain (i.e., our problem) will be removed "'not by might, nor by power, but by my Spirit,' says the LORD Almighty." We must diligently study Scripture to understand its meaning. Then we must explain it to our children and exhort them to put their trust in Jesus Christ alone for their salvation. Additionally, we must share God's word with all the people of the earth. In Matthew 28:19-20 Jesus commanded, "Therefore go and make disciples of all nations, baptizing them in the name of the Father and of the Son and of the Holy Spirit, and teaching them to obey everything I have commanded you."

Why were God's words written down? For the same reason God dried up the Jordan: "He did this so that all the peoples of the earth might know that the hand of the LORD is powerful and so that you might always fear the LORD your God" (Josh. 4:24). The apostle John tells us that is why he wrote his gospel: "These are written that you may believe that Jesus is the Christ, the Son of God, and that by believing you may have life in his name" (John 20:31). That was the purpose of the stone memorial, and that is the purpose of the Scriptures—

that we might come to know God through faith in the Lord Jesus Christ, and be saved.

Jesus Christ, Our Problem-Solver

God gave the Israelites a Joshua to lead them in triumph across the Jordan. But we have one who is greater than Joshua, the Lord Jesus Christ, who solved our greatest problem by means of his perfect life, death, and resurrection. We are sinners, subject to the infinite wrath of God, hell-bound, and hopeless in ourselves. Jesus solved our insoluble problem by suffering hell in our place on the cross. This glorious truth was foreshadowed by the ark of the Testimony and the annual Day of Atonement.

In Leviticus 16 we read that on the Day of Atonement, the high priest entered the Holy of Holies, the innermost sanctuary of the tabernacle, where stood the ark of the covenant. He sprinkled the blood of a goat, slain as a sin offering for the people, upon the cover of the ark, known as the mercy seat. The sprinkled blood prevented the all-holy God, who dwelt above this mercy seat, from seeing the tablets of the law inside the ark—a law that condemned the people as sinners. The death of the sacrificial animal satisfied God's perfect justice; he could now show mercy to his people and forgive their sin. This Old Testament ceremony thus pointed to the death of the Messiah, the suffering servant, whose shed blood alone atones for our guilt.

Only Jesus Christ can propitiate, or turn away, the just wrath of God against us. Now God is propitious to us; his favor rests upon us, because his wrath was put upon another. Having been reconciled to God through Jesus Christ, we can pass safely through every problem, every Jordan. Nothing in all creation can destroy us. We are with Christ and in Christ. He has destroyed death for us, liberating us from the fear of death, so that we can say with the apostle Paul, "Where, O death, is your victory? Where, O death, is your sting? The sting of death is sin, and the power of sin is the law. But thanks be to God! He gives us the victory through our Lord Jesus Christ" (1 Cor. 15:55–57). Those who trust in Jesus Christ will not drown in the Jordan but will walk through on dry ground.

People of God, let us go forward in life, knowing God is with us! Yes, we will face the Jordan, but fear not. The ark of the covenant is with us; let us look to it and follow it. With our God, we will soon cross our final Jordan and enter the promised land. So be not afraid, but be courageous; God will surely solve all our problems. Let us move forward, looking unto Jesus, the author and finisher of our faith, who will bring us into his presence, where we will dwell with him forever in everlasting joy!

5

Captain of the Lord's Army

Joshua 5

*Now when Joshua was near Jericho, he looked up and saw
a man standing in front of him with a drawn sword in his
hand. Joshua went up to him and asked, "Are you for us or
for our enemies?"*

*"Neither," he replied, "but as commander of the army of the
LORD I have now come." Then Joshua fell facedown to the
ground in reverence, and asked him, "What message does
my Lord have for his servant?"*

*The commander of the LORD's army replied, "Take off your
sandals, for the place where you are standing is holy." And
Joshua did so.*

Joshua 5:13–15

Joshua and the Israelites had witnessed
the wonderful, miracle-working power of God on their
behalf in the parting of the Jordan. They had memorialized
that day in keeping with God's command. Now, with the
river behind them, Joshua was already looking ahead,
considering the next problem. As Israel's general, he would

need to answer the challenge posed by the fortified walls of Jericho that towered before him.

As he approached the city to examine the situation more closely, Joshua discovered someone else already there—a man with a drawn sword in his hand. Not recognizing this warrior, and in an attempt to assess what danger or aid he might represent, Joshua asked, "Are you for us or for our enemies?" The man gave a peculiar answer. "Neither, but as the commander of the army of the LORD I have now come." Receiving this answer, Joshua immediately fell down to pay him homage, for he knew this awesome warrior was God himself.

In considering this encounter, we must carefully examine three particulars: the captain's sword, his self-identification, and his stipulation. Then we, like Joshua, must fall facedown at the feet of Jesus Christ, who is the great captain of the Lord's army.

The Sword

The first thing Joshua noticed about this stranger was his sword. It was drawn from the scabbard, ready for combat. We must be very clear in our thinking and rid ourselves of the notion of a sweet and beautiful Jesus, as if he were still a baby in a manger. Here we find the pre-incarnate Jesus, sword drawn, ready to judge the people of Canaan, a people whose iniquity was full.

There are at least two other instances in the Old Testament where the pre-incarnate Jesus, also known as "the angel of the LORD," appears in judgment. Earlier in Israel's history, the prophet Balaam had acquiesced to Balak's request to put a curse on God's people (Num. 22). As Balaam was traveling toward the camp of the Israelites to pronounce a curse upon them, God was very angry with him. We read in Numbers 22:31 that "the LORD opened Balaam's eyes, and he saw the angel of the LORD standing in the road with his sword drawn." This same angel of the Lord later visited God's judgment on the people of Israel, causing seventy thousand of them to die by plague. Before the plague was arrested, King David beheld the terrible sight of the angel of the Lord with his hand outstretched to destroy the city of Jerusalem (2 Sam. 24:16–17). We need to change our view of Jesus Christ. He saves, but he also judges.

Jesus Christ wields a sword in the New Testament as well. In the first scene of the book of Revelation, John the apostle relates his vision of the risen Lord and describes him this way: "His head and hair were white like wool, as white as snow, and his eyes were like blazing fire. His feet were like bronze glowing in a furnace, and his voice was like the sound of rushing waters. In his right hand he held seven stars, and out of his mouth came a sharp double-edged sword" (Rev. 1:14–16). When the apostle saw this, he fell down as though dead. Later, in the climactic battle scene of Revelation, Jesus is depicted as a victorious warrior, meting out the wrath of God (Rev. 19:11-16). Verse 15 says, "Out of his mouth comes a sharp sword with which to strike down the nations." The Lord Jesus Christ will strike down every kingdom, city, or person opposed to his rule. Jesus conquers all his enemies. We need to adjust our view of him!

The Self-Identification

The man then identified himself in response to Joshua's inquiry, "Are you for us or for our enemies?" "Neither," he replied, "but as commander of the army of the LORD I have now come." What is the significance of such an answer? It indicates that Jesus Christ cannot be recruited. He is God Himself. He is Savior and Judge. He does not answer to us; we answer to him. We may not enlist God for our projects, but he may enlist us in his.

Yet how many people come up with their own ideas and then ask God to bless them! Let us avoid reductionism, reducing God into someone who will cooperate with our plans, someone we can control. He is the commander, and we must surrender to him. We may want to adjust his word, but we cannot. This King of kings requires our complete surrender. In this surrender lies our salvation.

Joshua's response to the warrior's declaration was correct: he fell facedown to the ground and worshiped. This act confirms that the mysterious man was in fact God himself. He could not have been an angel, because angels do not accept worship. In Revelation 22:9 an angel rejects the apostle John's worship, saying, "Do not do it! I am a fellow servant with you. . . . Worship God!" But Joshua was not rebuked for this act of obeisance, for this man was not merely man nor even an angel, but the Second Person of the Trinity. He was the one who appeared to Moses in the burning bush (Exod. 3), who visited Abraham and warned him about Sodom's judgment (Gen. 18), and who wrestled with Jacob and put his hip out of its socket (Gen. 32).

When we understand who Jesus is, we will immediately fall down in reverence and surrender to him. If you have not done that, you have neither seen him nor known him. What we need is true knowledge of God. Otherwise, we will try to manipulate and recruit him for our personal plans. He is the commander of the army of the Lord. He governs us.

The Stipulation

The moment Joshua realized who was speaking to him, he asked, "What message does my Lord have for his servant?" In reply, the Lord gave Joshua this command: "Take off your sandals, for the place where you are standing is holy." Now Canaan was a most defiled place, a place whose iniquity was filled to overflowing. How, then, could this plot of ground be holy? Because God was present. God gave precisely the same command to Moses from the burning bush: "Do not come any closer. Take off your sandals, for the place where you are standing is holy ground" (Exod. 3:5). It is the presence of the holy God that makes a place holy. Joshua understood the seriousness of this directive. He obeyed without hesitation, as the text says simply: "And Joshua did so."

Joshua's encounter with the captain of the Lord's army is similar to that of Saul of Tarsus centuries later (Acts 9). Saul was on his way to Damascus to imprison the Christians of that city, when suddenly he was thrown from his donkey by a blinding light from heaven. From the dust he asked, "Who are you, Lord?" The Lord replied, "I am Jesus, whom you are persecuting. Now get up and go into the city, and you will be told what you must do." Saul then proceeded to Damascus, not to persecute the church, but to become God's servant in building it.

We, too, must first ask the same question that Joshua and Saul of Tarsus asked: "Who are you, Lord?" We need to know who this divine commander is. And, like Joshua and Saul, our second question must be, "What do you want me to do?" Once we have real knowledge of who God is, our concern will be to do his will. There will be no more argument. We will worship and serve him for life.

God demands that we surrender to him and render complete obedience to him. Yes, Jesus is the Savior, and, praise God, he saves sinners! But may we never forget that he is also Lord. He is the supreme commander of the heavenly hosts, and he wields a drawn sword. Let us therefore heed the warning of Psalm 2:12: "Kiss the Son, lest he be angry and you be destroyed in your way, for his wrath can flare up in a moment. Blessed are all who take refuge in him."

6

Faith Is the Victory That Overcomes the World

Joshua 6

*Now Jericho was tightly shut up because of the Israelites.
No one went out and no one came in. Then the LORD said
to Joshua, "See, I have delivered Jericho into your hands,
along with its king and its fighting men."*

Joshua 6:1–2

*By faith the walls of Jericho fell, after the people had
marched around them for seven days.*

Hebrews 11:30

We have seen in Joshua 3 and 4 how
the Lord miraculously parted the Jordan River, allowing
the people to cross from one side to the other. Chapter
5 begins by relating how the Israelite men, in obedience
to God's command, underwent circumcision, a covenant
obligation symbolizing Christian baptism (cf. Gen. 17:1–14;
Col. 2:11–15). By this the Israelites declared that they were

not autonomous, but belonged to God as his covenant people. After this, they enjoyed fellowship with God by observing the Passover, a festival prefiguring the New Testament ordinance of the Lord's Supper (cf. Exod. 12; Luke 22:7–20; 1 Cor. 11:23–26). In this celebration, the Israelites commemorated how God had delivered them from Egyptian bondage to be his holy people.

The Israelites had indeed begun well, but it was only a beginning; the Lord had much more in mind for them to accomplish in the land of Canaan. In the same way, the Christian life involves more than simply confessing Christ, being baptized, and taking Holy Communion. We are people of God, and so we have battles to fight and Jerichos to conquer, as our Lord commands us. Christians are not to be passive, complacent, and retreating. The Christian life is not a life of ease; we face conflict until we arrive in heaven. But take courage! The captain of the Lord's army is with us. And just as he dried up the Red Sea and the mighty Jordan, so will he fight against Jericho and all the cities of Canaan. He will defeat all our enemies, for they are his enemies as well.

By Faith We Are Confident

As the people of God, we have reason for great confidence. For God has delivered us from our bondage to sin and given us the victory of Christ, who conquered even death. But we cannot enjoy that victory unless we believe and obey him. We read in the First Epistle of John, "This is the victory that has overcome the world, even our faith" (1 John 5:4). By faith we wholly trust in the living and true God and in his promises. And by faith we obey God's commands exactly, immediately, and with great delight. People with this kind of faith will experience victory.

When Joshua succeeded Moses as the new leader of Israel, God said to him, "Be strong and very courageous. Be careful to obey all the law my servant Moses gave you. . . . Do not be terrified" (Josh. 1:7, 9). We cannot enjoy victory unless we believe and do what God tells us. If our faith in Christ is true faith, we will obey his commands, and as a result, the walls of Jericho will collapse before our eyes.

Because we repose our complete trust in God, we are confident in his promises, and know that the enemies we face have already been defeated. The apostle Paul tells us that Jesus Christ, "having disarmed the powers and authorities . . . made a public spectacle of them, triumphing over them by the cross" (Col. 2:15). In light of Christ's accomplishments, Paul exhorts us to "be strong in the Lord and in his mighty power. Put on the full armor of God so that you can take your stand against the devil's schemes. For our struggle is not against flesh and blood, but against the rulers, against the authorities, against the powers of this dark world and against the spiritual forces of evil in the heavenly realms" (Eph. 6:10–12). Notice the repetition of the word "against." We have many enemies—the devil, the sin within us, and the world—and we must take our stand against them, but we do so knowing that Jesus Christ is already the victor. If we resist the devil while standing firm in our faith, he will flee from us.

Let us now consider for a moment the challenge that Joshua and Israel faced. The ancient city of Jericho was located ten miles northwest of the Dead Sea. It was built on approximately ten acres of land, and thus it would have taken less than thirty minutes to walk around the city once. Nevertheless, it was a mighty fortress surrounded by thick, towering walls and bolted gates that protected its pagan inhabitants. The Israelites, however, were not to fear this great fortress or its inhabitants. In fact, we have read how all the Canaanite nations, including the people of Jericho, were terrified by the Israelites and their God—and for good reason! In Joshua 2 we saw Rahab confiding in the

Israelite spies, "When we heard of [how God dried up the Red Sea], our hearts melted and everyone's courage failed because of you, for the Lord your God is God in heaven above and on the earth below" (v. 11). God's miraculous parting of the Jordan added to the Canaanites' dread: "Now when all the Amorite kings west of Jordan and all the Canaanite kings along the coast heard how the Lord had dried up the Jordan before the Israelites until we had crossed over, their hearts melted and they no longer had the courage to face the Israelites" (Josh. 5:1).

Satan wants us to fear our enemies, but we must not be afraid—we are to trust in God. The king of Jericho determined to oppose the heavenly captain of the Lord's army. He had the gates of Jericho shut tightly against the Lord and his people. But the Lord marches on, and he will never be defeated. He goes ever forward; who can resist him? At his coming, the Red Sea divides, the Jordan dries up, and mighty Amorite kings are utterly defeated. How can the gates of Jericho prevail against him? Every opposition must fall before the almighty Lord of hosts.

So we read in Joshua 6:2: "The Lord said to Joshua, 'See, I have delivered Jericho into your hands, along with its king and its fighting men.'" Yes, we are called to fight, but it is God who gives the victory.

By Faith We Hear His Voice

How was Joshua to defeat this fortified city with its great walls? As a proven military leader, he could have considered a number of reasonable strategies—ladders, battering rams, tunnels, siege works. But Christians are commanded, "Trust in the Lord with all your heart and lean not onto your own understanding; in all your ways acknowledge him, and he will make your paths straight" (Prov. 3:5–6). We are not to solve problems by relying on our own understanding. Rather, by faith we hear from

God as he directs us by his Spirit through his word. He is sovereign, all-knowing, and personal. He communicates with his people and tells them what to do.

God's command to Joshua was for the people to march around the city during the seven days of the Feast of Unleavened Bread. When the wall collapsed, the people were to rush straight into the city from every direction. No ladders, no battering rams, no tunnel, no siege—just marching. It sounds like nonsense, but it was the word of the Lord. And when we believe God's word and are careful to do all that he commands, we will have complete victory.

We must listen carefully to our commander's instructions, for we are engaged in the Lord's war, not ours. In Isaiah 55:8 God tells us, "For my thoughts are not your thoughts, neither are your ways my ways." How many times have we listened to our own counsel or sought counsel from others, but not sought the counsel of the Lord? The way of God seems foolish to most people, whose thinking is based in human wisdom. But to us who believe, it is the power of God unto salvation (1 Cor. 1:18).

By Faith We Obey His Word

God said, "March around the city once a day for six days." As we noted, this would take about thirty minutes each day. Then he said, "On the seventh day, march around the city seven times." These were very specific commands, lacking any discernible military strategy, yet Joshua was expected to obey them. We must never try to manipulate, negotiate, delay, or deny the word of God. By faith we obey God's commands in every detail. First Samuel 15:22 tells us, "Does the LORD delight in burnt offerings and sacrifices as much as in obeying the voice of the LORD? To obey is better than sacrifice, and to heed is better than the fat of rams." We will never see victory until we operate on the basis of faith expressed in obedience to God.

God requires *orderly obedience*. The Israelites could not simply march in any manner they chose. God told them exactly how to advance. Armed men with swords in hand were to lead the procession. Behind them marched the priests, continually blowing the jubilee trumpets, as though announcing the coming of the king. Next came the ark, carried on the shoulders of the priests, and finally the rear guard, also armed with swords. That was the order established by God, and if Joshua or the people of Israel had changed it, God would have been displeased, and there would have been no victory. We also must carefully obey God's commands if we hope to experience his victory.

God requires *disciplined obedience*. He commanded the people of Israel to march silently around Jericho—they must not speak (6:10). One of the most difficult things for people to do is to keep their mouths shut. Scripture speaks of the impossibility of disciplining the tongue (James 3:6–8). Yet here these people were told, "You may not speak even one word." Can you imagine thousands upon thousands of people walking together without speaking a single word? Such discipline comes from the fear of the Lord, produced in the believer by the Spirit of God.

God requires *comprehensive obedience*. Joshua gave this instruction about the plunder from the conquest of Jericho: "All the silver and gold and the articles of bronze and iron are sacred to the LORD and must go into his treasury" (Josh. 6:19). Jericho was the firstfruits of the victory for God's people in Canaan, so the city and everything in it were to be devoted to the Lord. God gave this clear warning: "Keep away from the devoted things so that you will not bring about your own destruction by taking any of them" (6:18). Every facet of the Israelite campaign was to be regulated by the word of God.

God requires *patient obedience*. The same Lord who created the whole universe simply by speaking a word could have defeated Jericho in an instant. Why, then, did he take seven days to bring down its walls? We must understand that God tests his people's faith. We cannot tell him how he should do things; he tells us what to do. We must believe and obey. We are by nature impatient, but God wants us to trust patiently as we wait for him to act. Then we will enjoy the victory that he achieves in our behalf.

Though the Lord revealed his entire plan to Joshua, it appears that Joshua told the people only what they needed to know for each day. This was a test of their faith and patience. The people believed and obeyed the word that came to them daily. Each day they circled the city once in the prescribed order, in the presence of the ark. Notice, the ark is spoken of nine times in this chapter, emphasizing the central importance of the presence of God. Each time they circled, nothing happened. The walls stood there, mocking them and challenging them to come in. This happened the first day, the second day, the third day, and so on.

On the seventh day everyone got up very early. It seems the people still did not know what would happen in the end. They were to circle seven times, and at the trumpet blast and at the command of Joshua, they were to give a great shout. They had been told, "Shout! For the LORD has given you the city" (6:16), but they did not know how it was going to be accomplished. God directed the people to circle the city a total of thirteen times in seven days. So they marched the eleventh time, the twelfth time—and nothing happened. But still they believed God's word.

The kingdom of God is on the move, coming to conquer and to save. His people are moving with him by faith expressed in obedience to his commands. Faith results in unity, not in autonomy, rebellion, disagreement, or negotiation. God's people are to obey and submit to God and his delegated agents. We see such order throughout chapter 6. Joshua brought the word of God to the priests and the people, and they did what God commanded. Faith is the victory! God said it, we believe it, and that settles it. No matter what the scientists and the psychologists and the philosophers say, we believe what God has spoken. So these people did not become weary. They trusted God, knowing that he who dried up the mighty Jordan was mighty to conquer Jericho.

Then, at the right time, on the thirteenth circling, the priests gave a long blast on the trumpets as a signal. Joshua, the visible commander, also gave a signal, and all the people shouted together. This was the shout of victory, as we read in Numbers 23:21: "No misfortune is seen in Jacob, no misery observed in Israel. The LORD their God is with them; the shout of the King is among them." What happened when God's people shouted? The walls of Jericho collapsed, and each man from every direction charged straight ahead into the city. They put everyone but Rahab and her family to death, and burned the city, according to God's command.

The Kindness and Severity of God

What a clear picture of the goodness and severity of God! We must keep both in mind. The judgment of God was long in coming for the Canaanites and the Amorites. In Genesis 15:16 God said to Abraham, "The sin of the Amorites has not yet reached its full measure." God allowed hundreds of years to pass while their iniquity increased and became full to overflowing. The inhabitants of Canaan were wicked idolaters who mocked the true God and his laws, which are written on every human heart. The Bible tells us that they knew the true God, for he reveals his divinity and power to all men through creation. But in their hearts, they suppressed the truth that was plain to them about God and refused to worship him. Instead, they worshiped demons and practiced all forms of lawlessness (Rom. 1:18–25). Finally the time came for God to judge them.

So we read that at God's command the Israelites "devoted the city to the LORD and destroyed with the sword every living thing in it—men and women, young and old, cattle, sheep and donkeys. . . . Then they burned the whole city and everything in it" (6:21, 24). What right does God have to do all this? He has every right, for he is the Lord, Creator, and Judge of all the earth, and everything he does is just. I hope we will get rid of our wrong views of Jesus Christ. We must tremble before him, the captain of the Lord's army, who stands in our midst with a drawn sword. Those who oppose him and refuse to submit to his rule will experience the full severity of his judgment.

This captain has a drawn sword in his hand. Do not try to remove it; it is impossible. But look again at his hands. They are the hands of the crucified Jesus, who received from God the Father the just punishment for the sins of all the elect of God. God is holy, but he is also love. He judges, but he also saves. At the very time that judgment was falling upon the inhabitants of Jericho, salvation was coming to Rahab and her family. Rahab was an Amorite, a wicked prostitute, but she received mercy because she put her faith in God. It was for her and for all the Rahabs of the world that Jesus died.

Paul wrote to the New Testament church at Rome, "Consider therefore the kindness and sternness of God: sternness to those who fell, but kindness to you, provided that you continue in his kindness" (Rom. 11:22). God is not a teddy bear or a mere figment of human imagination. He is the omnipotent, self-existent God. The Bible says, "The wrath of God is being revealed from heaven against all the godlessness and wickedness of men who suppress the truth by their wickedness" (Rom. 1:18). Yet the same chapter also tells us that a righteousness from God is being revealed in the gospel for the salvation of everyone who believes (vv. 16–17).

Therefore, just as the priests continually sounded the trumpets while marching around the city, let us continually proclaim the good news of the gospel, announcing the coming of Jesus Christ, the King. He has come to save every Rahab who surrenders to him. Thus we declare, "Believe on the Lord Jesus Christ and you will be saved." These words may sound foolish and offensive to some people, but to those whose hearts God is opening, they are words of great deliverance. It is only those who surrender to Jesus Christ, the captain of the Lord's army, who will give a mighty shout of victory.

Faith Is the Victory

What, then, must we do? March on with God. Live by faith—a faith that confidently trusts in him, that hears his voice in his word, and that obeys every one of his commands. Study God's word and trust him implicitly. As God's people, we have been delivered from our bondage to sin and are triumphant in the victory of Christ. If you are living a defeated life, then listen to the word of God, believe and obey it, and you will be delivered. It is the destiny of the church to be triumphant. The city of man will fall, but the city of God will stand forever. Faith is the victory that overcomes the world!

7

Sin in the Church

Joshua 7

But the Israelites acted unfaithfully in regard to the devoted things; Achan son of Carmi, the son of Zimri, the son of Zerah, of the tribe of Judah, took some of them. So the LORD's anger burned against Israel.

Joshua 7:1

The sixth chapter of Joshua presented us with a marked contrast: joyful victory for God's covenant people, but utter destruction for his enemies who refuse to repent of their sins. Sadly, though, it is not just God's enemies who stubbornly resist him. Chapter 7 of Joshua teaches us about the reality of sin in the church—that people who profess to believe in God can also cherish sin in their hearts. And when they do, they discover that the One who was the enemy of Jericho has become their enemy as well.

Every Christian has entered into a covenant relationship with the Lord God Almighty. We have promised to honor him, believe him, and obey him. When we are faithful to these promises, we experience his presence and blessing.

But when we violate the covenant through unbelief and disobedience, we suffer inevitable loss. These principles are central to God's covenant relationship with his people and are operative in the church today just as they were in the time of Joshua.

The Reality of Sin in the Church

The story of Achan is the story of a believer who would not give up sin. A member of the tribe of Judah, Achan had participated in all the events recorded in Joshua 1–6. Together with the other Israelites, he had stood at the threshold of the promised land and agreed to fully obey God. Achan had crossed the Jordan with them on dry ground. He had been circumcised, receiving the sign of the covenant in his body. He had celebrated the Passover with the community, signifying his fellowship with God and with them. He had marched with the Israelite soldiers for seven days around the walls of Jericho with a sword in his hand. When the great walls fell, he was with those who stormed the city, meting out God's judgment upon its citizens. Achan had participated in all these events. In every way he appeared to be a covenant keeper.

Yet Achan sinned against the Lord of the covenant. God had given this command and warning to his people concerning the plunder from their victory over Jericho: "Keep away from the devoted things, so that you will not bring about your own destruction by taking any of them. Otherwise you will make the camp of Israel liable to destruction and bring trouble on it. All the silver and gold and the articles of bronze and iron are sacred to the LORD and must go into his treasury" (Josh. 6:18–19). But Achan contravened the Lord's command. He coveted and stole from among the spoils a beautiful Babylonian robe, two hundred shekels of silver, and a wedge of gold weighing fifty shekels. Then he hid them in the ground inside his tent (7:21). Though willing to wage war against sinful Jericho, he refused to subdue the sin in his own heart.

Achan's tragic fall is worthy of careful examination, for it is symbolic of sin's course. First, Achan saw, and he did not avert his gaze. Then he allowed covetousness to take hold of his heart and make him a captive to sin. James, the brother of Jesus, describes the downward spiral of sin in these words: "Each one is tempted when, by his own evil desire, he is dragged away and enticed. Then, after desire has conceived, it gives birth to sin; and sin, when it is full-grown, gives birth to death" (James 1:14–15).

We find other examples of this progression of sin elsewhere in the Scriptures: Eve fell into the same trap when she ate from the forbidden tree in the Garden of Eden—she saw the tree's good fruit, she coveted it, and she took it (Gen. 3:6). King David transgressed in a similar manner when he committed adultery with Bathsheba— he gazed down from his rooftop at her, lusted after her, and took her (2 Sam. 11). Sinful action is always first conceived and nurtured in the heart.

Furthermore, instead of repenting of this wicked act, Achan and his family attempted to hide it by burying the devoted things under the floor of their tent. They refused to confess or repent. It was only when the omniscient Lord singled them out that they admitted what they had done.

Every time God's people say yes to sin, they experience loss. If we persistently refuse to confess and forsake our sin, we bring increasing judgment on ourselves. The apostle Paul warned the Corinthian Christians, "That is why many among you are weak and sick, and a number of you have fallen asleep [i.e., died]" (1 Cor. 11:30). Sin wants to destroy us, but we must master it. We must honor God's word when it is spoken to us and not give way to temptation. If we do sin, we must quickly and truly repent, confess our sin, and forsake it.

The Reason for Sin in the Church

How could Achan have committed this theft when God had spoken a specific word against it? By first committing in his heart the sin of reductionism—remaking God in his own mind as a lesser being. By reducing God, Achan could then steal and hide the treasures from Jericho, believing that God would not be able to see them. Whenever we sin, we reject God's omnipresence, omnipotence, and omniscience. We create God after our own image, and persuade ourselves that he cannot detect our sin. Such is the perversity of the human heart.

But God is "Jehovah Jireh." These Hebrew words mean "God who sees." He is the God who sees our needs and provides for them, as well as the God who sees our sins and judges us. Not only does he see our external deeds, but he also sees the covetousness in our hearts. He sees our thoughts. God, who sees all things, exposed Achan's sin. We may succeed in deceiving human beings, but we can never fool God.

The Results of Sin in the Church

What were the results of Achan's sin? After their decisive victory over Jericho, the Israelites were confident as they proceeded to fight against the nearby city of Ai. Joshua sent only three thousand soldiers, expecting them to easily take the city. But victory turned to defeat—the Israelites were routed by a small force of men at Ai, and thirty-six Israelites were killed. This was Israel's first defeat in the land of Canaan, and it caused their hearts to melt like water. The entire community was shocked, confused, and dismayed. Even Joshua began to doubt. But the Lord, in great mercy, revealed to Joshua the reason for such a disastrous outcome: "Israel has sinned; they have violated my covenant, which I commanded them to keep.

They have taken some of the devoted things; they have stolen, they have lied, they have put them with their own possessions. That is why the Israelites cannot stand against their enemies" (Josh. 7:11–12).

When a member of God's community deliberately sins and refuses to repent, God withdraws his blessing. The individual, his family, and his church all suffer loss. In this sense, Achan's sin was not only against the Lord of the covenant, but also against his fellow Israelites. Joshua 7:1 gives solemn expression to this truth: "But the Israelites acted unfaithfully in regard to the devoted things; Achan son of Carmi, the son of Zimri, the son of Zerah, of the tribe of Judah, took some of them. So the Lord's anger burned against Israel." Because one man sinned, all Israel suffered. Although we come to God as individuals, we are not autonomous; we are connected to one another. When one rejoices, everyone rejoices. When one suffers, everyone suffers. When one sins, everyone loses.

Because of Achan's sin, the Israelites were defeated at Ai. Yet there is a more terrible consequence of sin: God withdraws his presence. God said to Joshua, "I will not be with you anymore unless you destroy whatever among you is devoted to destruction" (Josh. 7:12). God is a holy God. He cannot ignore sin, nor can he dwell with it. There is no greater curse than the withdrawal of God's presence from our lives, from our families, or from our church. If God is not with us, we cannot be blessed: our prayers are not heard, we experience confusion, and we are made liable to destruction. How Joshua must have trembled when God said to him, "I will not be with you anymore."

The Remedy for Sin in the Church

Achan and his family continued to conceal their sin, even after the devastating defeat at Ai. So God commanded the Israelites to consecrate themselves in preparation for his coming judgment, and then to present themselves to him. God said, "He who is caught with the devoted things shall be destroyed by fire, along with all that belongs to him" (Josh. 7:15). Early the next morning, as the tribes were assembled, God singled out first the tribe of Judah, then the clan of the Zerahites, then the family of Zimri, and finally Achan, son of Carmi, the son of Zimri. Achan was discovered by divine direction and detection.

At Joshua's prompting, Achan confessed his sin. Was this true confession? No. He had been caught, and although he confessed, he remained unrepentant. So the Israelites retrieved the stolen goods from his tent, and according to the Lord's command, they took Achan, his family, the stolen goods, and all that he owned to the Valley of Achor, which means Valley of Trouble. Joshua asked Achan, "Why have you brought this trouble on us? The LORD will bring trouble on you today" (Josh. 7:25). Then they stoned Achan and his family and all that they owned. They burned them and heaped up a large pile of rocks over them.

Forgiveness was not extended to Achan and his family because they were guilty of high-handed sin. They knew the Lord's command, but did not care. They stole, lied, concealed, and refused to repent. Even when all Israel suffered because of their sin, they were unmoved. And God was angry with the entire nation of Israel. What was the remedy for such a situation? God himself provided the remedy: "You cannot stand against your enemies until you remove it" (Josh. 7:13). Both the sin and the unrepentant sinner must be removed.

The Israelites dealt decisively with sin by the means God had prescribed for them. So the last verse in Joshua 7 states, "Then the LORD turned from his fierce anger." Moreover, God's blessing returned to the Israelites. The next chapter begins, "Then the LORD said to Joshua, 'Do not be afraid; do not be discouraged.'" The Lord then guided them in battle against Ai and they won a great victory.

How Should We Then Live?

God's covenant relationship with his people remains the same throughout all generations, and God has given his church clear instructions regarding sin and sinners. First, we must wage war against the sin in our own hearts on a daily basis. Christ's atoning work on the cross has set us free from the power of sin, so we are able to exercise dominion over the sin within us. It is particularly important that each Christian renounce all secret sins immediately. Understand that unconfessed sin hurts not only you, but your family and your church as well. On the other hand, if we confess our sins, God is faithful and just and will forgive us our sins and purify us from all unrighteousness (1 John 1:9).

Second, it is our responsibility to watch out for our brothers and sisters in the church. Each of us must rebuke, correct, and help one another to do what is right. We cannot ignore obvious sin, for it destroys both the sinner and the community. When our brother or sister repents, we must be quick to forgive (Luke 17:3–4). When someone persists in sin, however, we must take other church members with us and confront that person (Matt. 18:16).

Finally, if a member of the church refuses to give up deliberate sin, remaining unrepentant and incorrigible even after being confronted by the church, then the community has a responsibility to put that person out (Matt. 18:17). Until such action is taken, God will not be present to bless.

Let us, then, walk carefully, making sure that no high-handed sin brings trouble to the church. God has given us the command to say no to sin and yes to righteousness by the power of the Holy Spirit. Let us therefore walk in the liberty of the children of God, that we and the entire community may enjoy God's blessings.

8

The Constitutional
Convention of Canaan

Joshua 8

*Joshua read all the words of the law—the blessings and
the curses—just as it is written in the Book of the Law.
There was not a word of all that Moses had commanded
that Joshua did not read to the whole assembly of Israel,
including the women and children, and the aliens who
lived among them.*

Joshua 8:34–35

The U.S. Constitution, created in 1787
to be the supreme law of the United States, is widely
held to be a superb construct. It was the product of the
collective genius of a group of uniquely gifted men. Yet
it remains a human document, and as such it cannot
compare with the Bible, which is the very word of God.
The Bible is the constitution of God's church, and the
constitutional convention attracting our interest in
this chapter is not the one held in 1787, but rather the
one convened in 1400 BC and recorded in the eighth
chapter of the book of Joshua.

The Constitutional Convention

The nation of Israel was to be a theocracy in which the covenant Lord ruled his people by his covenant word. In Deuteronomy 27 the Lord commanded Moses what the Israelites should do to inaugurate this theocratic kingdom after they crossed the Jordan River and entered the promised land. In fulfillment of his command, Joshua gathered the people of Israel together and held a constitutional convention in celebration of God's law. Let us examine six elements of this first constitutional convention, and consider their relevance for Christians today.

1. THE PARTICIPANTS
All the people of God in Israel attended this gathering—no one was exempt. Joshua 8:33 tells us: "All Israel, aliens and citizens alike, with their elders, officials and judges, were standing on both sides of the ark of the covenant of the LORD," and in verse 35 we are told that Joshua read God's law "to the whole assembly of Israel, including the women and children, and the aliens who lived among them." All of God's people were required to hear and agree to God's word as the governing rule in their life and society.

2. THE LOCATION
In Deuteronomy 11 and 27 the Lord prescribed where the inauguration of the theocracy was to take place. Two barren mountains stood in central Canaan, Mount Ebal to the north and Mount Gerizim to the south. Between these mountains lay the Valley of Shechem, about five hundred yards wide. This formation of mountains and narrow valley resulted in a vast natural amphitheater with excellent acoustic qualities, so that what was spoken on one mountain could be heard clearly on the other as well as on the valley floor.

The Valley of Shechem was a significant location in Israelite history. Six hundred years before the time of Joshua, Abraham built an altar there to the Lord and offered sacrifices in response to a theophany in which the Lord promised him children and land (Gen. 12:6–7). After returning from Mesopotamia with his family, Abraham's grandson Jacob bought a plot of land in Shechem for one hundred pieces of silver and built an altar there, calling it El Elohe, the God of Israel (Gen. 33:18–20). There he also dug a well, which came to be known as "Jacob's well." Centuries later a Samaritan woman would have a life-changing encounter with Jesus at this well (John 4:1–42). It was in Shechem that Jacob's daughter Dinah was defiled, provoking her brothers Simeon and Levi to kill the people of Shechem and take the spoils (Gen. 34). Shechem was the place where Jacob's son Joseph went to look for his brothers (Gen. 37:14), and where he was later buried (Josh. 24:32). Not only did the first constitutional convention of Israel take place in Shechem, as described in Joshua 8, but also the last one, as recorded in Joshua 24.

3. THE LAW

The law of the covenant Lord was the constitution of God's theocratic kingdom. Through Moses, the Lord had instructed Joshua to write all the words of the law on whitewashed stone pillars that stood about six to eight feet high. So we read in Joshua 8:32, "There, in the presence of the Israelites, Joshua copied on stones the law of Moses, which he had written."

Not only did Joshua write the law on stone pillars for the people to read, but he also declared it publicly to them. All the Israelites—thousands of men, women, children, and aliens—listened as the entire word of the Lord was read aloud: "There was not a word of all that Moses had commanded that Joshua did not read to the whole assembly of Israel" (v. 35).

What was the responsibility of the people in response to this reading of the law? They were to agree with it, just as their forefathers did in Exodus 24:7: "Ther [Moses] took the Book of the Covenant and read it to the people. They responded, 'We will do everything the LORD has said; we will obey.'"

And so by God's command, six tribes now stood on Mount Gerizim and six on Mount Ebal. The tribes of Reuben, Zebulun, Gad, Asher, Dan, and Naphtali pronounced the twelve curses of Deuteronomy 27:15–26 from Mount Ebal, and the people responded, "Amen." By this response, they were in effect saying, "We accept the constitution of this theocracy, and if we fail to obey it, may God's curse fall on us." The tribes of Simeon, Levi, Judah, Issachar, Joseph, and Benjamin stood on Mount Gerizim, the mountain of blessing, and read words of blessing from the Book of the Law, probably those recorded in Deuteronomy 28:1–14. Again the people responded with an "amen" at the reading of each blessing, accepting the word of the covenant Lord, and acknowledging that they would be blessed if they obeyed it.

How does God's law differ from the constitutions of human governments? Human constitutions are written by men and result from collaboration and compromise, but God's law comes to us straight from heaven. Paul the apostle describes this unique quality of God's word: "All Scripture is God-breathed and is useful for teaching, rebuking, correcting and training in righteousness, so that the man of God may be thoroughly equipped for every good work" (2 Tim. 3:16). Peter tells us, "Above all, you must understand that no prophecy of Scripture came about by the prophet's own interpretation. For prophecy never had its origin in the will of man, but men spoke from God as they were carried along by the Holy Spirit" (2 Pet. 1:20–21). Human constitutions are based upon the interpretations of men, but God's constitution is the result of heavenly revelation.

4. THE ALTAR

The Lord also instructed Joshua to build an altar at the base of Mount Ebal, the mountain of curse. This altar was to be built of undressed, natural fieldstones. What was the symbolism of these uncut stones? According to Francis Schaeffer, no human skill was to be used on these altar stones because the Lord detests any demonstration of human self-righteousness (*Joshua and the Flow of Biblical History*, 120–126).

Why was the altar of sacrifice placed at the foot of Mount Ebal instead of Mount Gerizim? Because all have violated God's law and are under a curse. Scripture tells us that "the wrath of God is being revealed from heaven against all the godlessness and wickedness of men who suppress the truth by their wickedness" (Rom. 1:18). It also declares that "there is no one righteous, not even one" (Rom. 3:10). This is true for all people, including the chosen people of God. Thus, we must first come to the foot of Mount Ebal and behold God's unchanging law as it is written upon the stones. And when we come to God's law, we must acknowledge our sin and guilt.

But where there is law, there is also grace. The Lord, who gave the law through Moses, also gave Aaron as high priest to offer sacrifices for the sins of his people. And he who spoke the law also commanded that an altar of undressed stones be built. What was the purpose of this altar? It was an altar of sacrifice, where atonement could be made for the sins of God's people.

5. THE SACRIFICES

A sinful, cursed people can have fellowship with God only through the sacrifice of a perfect substitute. Deuteronomy 27:26 says, "Cursed is the man who does not uphold the words of this law by carrying them out." We are required to obey all of the law all of the time. Yet the truth is that we do not. But thanks be to God, "Christ redeemed us from the curse of the law by becoming a curse for us" (Gal. 3:13). Jesus Christ was crucified on a cross as the cursed one in our place. "God made him who had no sin to be sin for us, so that in him we might become the righteousness of God" (2 Cor. 5:21).

Because we all are sinners, we must first come to Mount Ebal, the mountain of law, curse, and sacrifice. We must confess our sins and put our faith in Christ's perfect sacrifice of reconciliation. Then our guilt is taken away—by grace we are saved through faith (Eph. 2:8). As we then live in covenant faithfulness to the constitution given to us in God's infallible, everlasting word, we enjoy the blessings declared from Mount Gerizim. In Galatians 3:14 we read, "[Christ] redeemed us"—that is, from the curse of the law—"in order that the blessing given to Abraham might come to [us] through Christ Jesus."

Self-righteous people reject God's order. They see no need for the cross of Christ; they think they deserve God's blessings solely on the basis of their own goodness. Paul diagnosed this problem of self-righteousness among the Jews of his day:

> What then shall we say? That the Gentiles, who did not pursue righteousness, have obtained it, a righteousness that is by faith; but Israel, who pursued a law of righteousness, has not attained it. Why not? Because they pursued it not by faith but as if it were by works. They stumbled over the "stumbling stone." As it is written: "See, I lay in Zion a stone that causes men to stumble and a rock that makes them fall, and the one who trusts in him will never be put to shame." Brothers, my heart's desire and prayer to God for the Israelites is that they may be saved. For I can testify about them that they are zealous for God, but their zeal is not based on knowledge. Since they did not know the righteousness that comes from God and

sought to establish their own, they did not submit to God's righteousness. Christ is the end of the law so that there may be righteousness for everyone who believes. (Rom. 9:30–10:4)

We come to the blessings of Mount Gerizim through the sacrifice at Mount Ebal. Without the cross of Christ there can be no crown of heaven.

6. THE ARK OF THE COVENANT

The ark of the covenant, carried by the priests and symbolizing the presence of God, was also there at the convention. The Lord never leaves nor forsakes his people; he is always in their midst. Just so, in Matthew 28:20 our Lord Jesus Christ promises us, "Surely I am with you always, to the very end of the age." This knowledge of God's presence with us should fill us with encouragement.

At the same time, the awareness of God's presence must also produce in us great sobriety. In Revelation 2 and 3 we read that the Lord is in the midst of his church, with eyes like blazing fire. Everything is laid bare in his presence. He is called the heart-knower (Acts 1:24, 15:8), for he knows our very thoughts. We may be able to deceive others—our parents or pastors or friends—but we can never deceive God.

The Lord was in the midst of his people in the Old Testament, and the Lord is in the midst of his church today. Jesus said, "For where two or three come together in my name, there am I with them" (Matt. 18:20). God is with us to bless all who obey him and to discipline all who do not.

Jesus at Shechem

Not only did Abraham, Jacob, Joseph, and Joshua go to Shechem, but Jesus, the greater Joshua, also went there fourteen hundred years later to speak with a Samaritan woman by Jacob's well (John 4).

The Samaritans had built a temple on Mount Gerizim, the mount of blessing, in the fourth century BC, and they worship on Mount Gerizim even today. This Samaritan woman, who had lived a life of sin, worshiped at Mount Gerizim, yet she had not acknowledged her violation of God's constitutional law. When she came to Jacob's well to get water, Jesus offered her the water of eternal life, that is, salvation. However, before she could drink of this water, she first had to confess and repent of her sins. Jesus refuses to save anyone who comes on the basis of his or her own righteousness; he saves only sinners.

So, Jesus told the woman to go and get her husband. This was a heart-searching demand by the heart-knower himself, intended to convict the woman of her sin. She correctly acknowledged that she had no husband, but still did not admit the sin that was carefully concealed in her statement. Jesus then exposed her whole life of sin: "You are right when you say you have no husband. The fact is, you have had five husbands, and the man you now have is not your husband" (John 4:17–18). As Christ's words cut her to her heart, she confessed and repented of her sins.

Then the woman went and told her fellow Shechemites, "Come, see a man who told me everything I ever did. Could this be the Christ?" (v. 29). Hearing this, many people from the city then came to Jesus and also confessed him as their Messiah and the Savior of the world. There is no salvation without first coming to Mount Ebal. There is no salvation without repentance. As the Messiah, Jesus gave the woman and her neighbors full forgiveness and eternal life on the basis of his soon-to-come, substitutionary sacrifice on Mount Calvary.

In Jesus Christ, the Word of God had come once again to Shechem and brought salvation. Jesus is the Lamb of God who takes away the sins of the world. He is the King of Israel, the covenant Lord, the mediator of the new covenant. He is the altar, the sacrifice, and the great high priest. And he is the King of the kingdom of God, who rules his church by his eternal, unchanging word.

The Constitution Today

The first constitutional convention at Shechem teaches us certain timeless truths: The Lord is the king of Israel; his word is the constitution of Israel; Israel must acknowledge her sin and receive salvation by grace through faith in the gift of sacrifice; and Israel's subsequent obedience results in blessing while her disobedience results in curse.

The Christian church is the Israel of God today, and we are still required to regulate our lives by the Lord's constitution, which is the completed canon of Scripture. Covenant people delight in the law of their Lord, and as we obey it, we will go from blessing to blessing.

Who are the people of God's covenant? They are those who join themselves to the covenant Lord through repentance and faith. "If you confess with your mouth, 'Jesus is Lord,' and believe in your heart that God raised him from the dead, you will be saved" (Rom. 10:9). So we must first come to Mount Ebal and look at the law to see our guilt. Then we must move to the altar and put our trust in the once-for-all perfect sacrifice of Jesus Christ. As we do so, he will forgive our sins as he forgave the sins of the Samaritan woman. Since all have violated God's law and are under a curse, the sacrifice of Christ is the only basis for our justification. "Therefore, there is now no condemnation for those who are in Christ Jesus" (Rom. 8:1). As the elect people of God, we will then be enabled by the Holy Spirit to obey the constitution of our Lord. We will delight in it, and we will enjoy the blessings of Mount Gerizim.

Why should we obey the heavenly constitution? Because the principle of blessing and cursing is eternally valid. As the Spirit pleaded through Moses, he still pleads with us today: "I have set before you life and death, blessings and curses. Now choose life" (Deut. 30:19).

Jesus Christ is coming again as Judge. He will purge all evil, and there will be a final excommunication of those who have refused to obey his constitution. Matthew's gospel tells us, "Then the King will say to those on his right, 'Come, you who are blessed by my Father; take your inheritance, the kingdom prepared for you since the creation of the world.' . . . Then he will say to those on his left, 'Depart from me, you who are cursed, into the eternal fire prepared for the devil and his angels.' . . . Then they will go away to eternal punishment, but the righteous to eternal life" (Matt. 25:34–46). We cannot wish away hell, judgment, or death, for these things are decreed in God's constitution.

Brothers and sisters, today I set before you life and death, blessing and cursing. May God's Holy Spirit motivate you to begin at Mount Ebal, so that you may understand that you have violated God's law and are under his wrath. Then fix your sight on the sacrifice made once-for-all at the cross of Mount Calvary. Christ became a curse in our place that we might become the righteousness of God. Trust in him and move from the mount of curse to the mount of blessing through faith in the Lord Jesus Christ. And if you profess to be a Christian but have been living a backslidden life, I exhort you to repent this very day. Look to Christ, who is in the midst of us to forgive, to heal, to comfort, to enlighten, and to empower.

9

When We Don't Pray

Joshua 9

The men of Israel sampled their provisions but did not inquire of the LORD.

Joshua 9:14

When we neglect prayer, we can be easily deceived and make wrong decisions. And when leaders do not pray, they harm not only themselves but also the people under them. The ninth chapter of Joshua speaks about the utter failure of Israel's leaders—Joshua, the princes of the twelve tribes, the priests, and the elders—to seek guidance from God when they were approached by the Gibeonites. Everyone who is responsible for making decisions—fathers, mothers, teachers, elders, or others—should pay careful attention to this chapter, for here we are given a clear picture of the problems God's people bring on themselves when they do not pray.

The Lord had given Joshua adequate instructions before he and the people entered Canaan. Joshua was to lead the Israelites into Canaan and give them rest by defeating all their enemies; he was to be strong and courageous; and he was to obey the entire word of God, not turning to the right or to the left. Joshua had the book of the law, the ark of the covenant, and the priests to consult the Urim and Thummin (Num. 27:21). He could recall how the Lord had answered Moses when he prayed. He himself had heard the voice of the Lord on many occasions (e.g., Joshua 1:1; 3:7; 4:1; 5:2; 6:2; 7:10; 8:1). His job was simply to hear from God and do his will in each new situation. Yet Joshua failed to do so at least two times. We want to examine these failures of Joshua so that we do not repeat them in our lives.

The First Failure of Joshua

Joshua first failed to seek the will of God in his campaign against the city of Ai (Josh. 7:1–8:29). The name "Ai" literally means "the heap" or "the ruin"; it was a small, insignificant city. Joshua sent out spies to bring back a report about Ai, but he did not inquire of the Lord. He made his decision based solely on the report of the spies, who said, "Not all the people will have to go up against Ai. Send two or three thousand men to take it and do not weary all the people, for only a few men are there" (Josh. 7:3). How eager we are to hear from people rather than God! As Christians, we say that Jesus Christ is our Lord, but we often act as though we are each self-determining lords. Though claiming to do God's will, we follow our own desires. The result is often disastrous.

The decision must have seemed so simple to Joshua. Not all the people would have to go. Had he inquired of the Lord, however, Joshua would have realized that God's will was very different than what the spies recommended. The Lord wanted him to take the whole army when he went to attack Ai (Josh. 8:1). Joshua was also completely unaware of Achan's idolatry and God's consequent displeasure with the Israelites. It was not until thirty-six soldiers died and Israel was defeated that Joshua finally "fell facedown to the ground before the ark of the LORD" (7:6). Only then did God reveal to the leaders the problem and his will in the matter. After Joshua obeyed by meting out judgment on Achan, God once again led his people in victory.

How many times have we neglected prayer or tried in our "prayers" to have God alter his eternal plan and accept ours! When someone asks if we have prayed about a matter, we quickly say yes. What we mean is, "Yes, I told God what he should do." But God does all things according to the counsel of his own sovereign will. As Christians, we are called to pray earnestly that we might know and do the will of God. We are to pray, "Thy kingdom come, thy will be done," and, "Not my will, but thine be done." We are to deny ourselves, take up the cross, and follow Christ daily.

The Second Failure of Joshua

Joshua's second failure is specifically mentioned in Joshua 9. Just a few miles southwest of Ai lay the city of Gibeon (modern El-Gib). The Gibeonites were Hivites whose iniquity, like that of the rest of the Canaanites, was full to overflowing. The Israelites were not to show them compassion by making a treaty with them, but were to exterminate all of them, for this was God's clearly revealed will. Deuteronomy 7:1–6 reveals the divine rationale for such extermination:

> When the LORD your God brings you into the land you are entering to possess and drives out before you many nations—the Hittites, Girgashites, Amorites, Canaanites, Perizzites, Hivites and Jebusites, seven nations larger and stronger than you—and when the LORD your God has delivered them over to you and you have defeated them, then you must destroy them totally. Make no treaty with them, and show them no mercy. Do not intermarry with them. Do not give your

daughters to their sons or take their daughters for your sons, for they will turn your sons away from following me to serve other gods, and the LORD's anger will burn against you and will quickly destroy you. This is what you are to do to them: Break down their altars, smash their sacred stones, cut down their Asherah poles and burn their idols in the fire. For you are a people holy to the LORD your God. The LORD your God has chosen you out of all the peoples on the face of the earth to be his people, his treasured possession.

Joshua knew this divine mandate. As the leader of God's people, he was supposed to read the word of God daily and obey all of it without adjusting it in any way. Surely he knew that the Scripture specifically prohibited making any covenant with the people of Canaan, including the Hivites (Exod. 23:32; 34:12; Deut. 7:2).

On the other hand, cities that were far from Canaan were to be spared from such destruction. Deuteronomy 20:10–11 gives instructions regarding these outlying cities: "When you march up to attack a city, make its people an offer of peace. If they accept and open their gates, all the people in it shall be subject to forced labor and shall work for you." The Gibeonites, who lived nearby, pretended to be from a far country, and thus were able to deceive Joshua and all the leaders of Israel into thinking that they were entitled to the favor of peace.

Why were these leaders deceived? Because they were walking by sight, not by faith. They leaned on their own understanding and did not seek the Lord's will. They failed to understand that reality does not consist solely in material things. If that were the case, we would only need sensory perception to make right decisions.

The Gibeonites came up with a ruse to fool Joshua. They brought worn-out sacks and old, cracked and mended wineskins, hoping that he would arrive at the conclusion that they had traveled a long distance. They deliberately wore patched sandals and threadbare clothes.

Their bread was dry, moldy and crumbling. Not only that, they declared, "We have come from a distant country; make a treaty with us" (9:6). Joshua and the other leaders questioned them, but not very thoroughly. Notice, the Gibeonites never volunteered their nationality or the name of their country. Instead, they carefully ingratiated themselves with the Israelites, feeding their pride by saying, "We are your servants. . . . We are your servants. . . . We are your servants. . . . Your God is great and we have heard of his fame."

Finally, the Gibeonites asked the leaders to verify the truth of their story by tasting their bread: "This bread of ours was warm when we packed it at home on the day we left to come to you. But now see how dry and moldy it is" (v. 12). This was the last empirical test proving that they had come from a distant land. The leaders tasted the bread, were convinced, and proceeded to make an inviolable treaty with the Gibeonites in the name of the Lord.

See how careful Joshua and the leaders were. They interrogated these people, listened closely to their story, observed their worn-out clothes and sandals, and tasted their bread. They did all these things. But they did not do the one thing they should have done—they did not seek the Lord. How true this is of us also! How often, when we are faced with serious decisions, will we do everything but speak to the One who knows everything.

When we make decisions based solely on our own observations and understanding, we are acting as though all reality is material, capable of being perceived and tested by smell, taste, touch, hearing, and sight. But there is a spiritual reality that includes God and his angels, as well as the devil and his demons. There is the kingdom of God and the kingdom of Satan. Paul speaks of this spiritual reality many times: "So we fix our eyes not on what is seen, but on what is unseen. For what is seen is temporary, but what is unseen is eternal" (2 Cor. 4:18), "For our struggle is not against flesh and blood, but against the rulers, against the authorities, against the powers of this dark world and against the spiritual forces of evil in the heavenly realms" (Eph. 6:12), and "We are not unaware of [Satan's] schemes" (2 Cor. 2:11).

Sadly, Joshua and the leaders *were* unaware of the schemes of their enemies, the Gibeonites. Why? "The men of Israel sampled their provisions but did not inquire of the LORD" (9:14). This was the key failure, the fatal flaw of these leaders—they acted on their own understanding and failed to inquire of the Lord. Notice the response of mighty Joshua when he realized he had been fooled: "Then Joshua summoned the Gibeonites and said, 'Why did you deceive us?'" (v. 22). Oh, what a sad question for a leader to ask! He should have asked, "Why was *I* deceived?"

The Danger of Being Deceived

As Christians, we are in constant danger of being deceived by the world, the flesh, and the devil. We cannot always judge situations properly; we must have God's help in order to know his will. Recall how the prophet Samuel almost anointed the wrong son of Jesse as king of Israel. When he saw Eliab, the firstborn, Samuel thought, "Surely the LORD's anointed stands here before the LORD" (1 Sam. 16:6). He was convinced that Eliab was the one God had chosen and was about to anoint him. "But the LORD said to Samuel, 'Do not consider his appearance or his height, for I have rejected him'" (v. 7). Samuel said, "He is the man!" But God said, "He is not the man. I have chosen another." Then God articulated a crucial principle: "The LORD does not look at the things man looks at. Man looks at the outward appearance, but the LORD looks at the heart." How many times have we made decisions based simply on outward appearance! We think, "That person is so good-looking and smart—what more could I want?" It is terrible to be fooled when we make such decisions, for not only do we have to live with the consequences, but so also do future generations.

Second Samuel 7 gives us another example of a man of God jumping to the wrong conclusion. When King David wanted to build a temple for God, the prophet Nathan told him, "Whatever you have in mind, go ahead and do it, for the LORD is with you" (v. 3). But that night the Lord told Nathan that David was not to build the temple. Even a prophet can make wrong decisions! Nathan initially gave King David incorrect counsel because he did not seek the Lord's will first.

Joshua and the leaders failed to consult the Scripture and obey it fully. Joshua had the Pentateuch, which gave specific directions about how he should receive guidance for matters not revealed in the Scripture. "He is to stand before Eleazar the priest, who will obtain decisions for him by inquiring of the Urim before the Lord" (Num. 27:21). Joshua neglected this Scripture, thus he failed to consult the priest who was there with the ark. The priest had the Urim and the Thummin, devices by which to find out the will of God. But Joshua failed to make use of this divine provision for guidance. He probably thought that it was obvious which way to go, and reasoned, "Why bother to go to God and to the Bible, when the choice is so clear?"

Deuteronomy 8:3 tells us we are to live by "every word that comes from the mouth of the LORD." We are not to rely on our own understanding, even when we think the direction is clear, for it may not be that certain. Joshua and the elders were duped because they did not seek the objective will of God. What failure! What tragedy! How terrible it is to make decisions based on carnal understanding. How easily we too can be deceived by appearances and conclude that we know God's will when, in fact, the will of God is the exact opposite! What we need is wisdom from above, so that we will not be fooled by the deceptions of the Gibeonites of the world, and of the church.

The Success of the Greater Joshua

Thanks be to God, there is One who is greater than Joshua—our Lord Jesus Christ. He was tempted by Satan, yet he triumphed by saying, "It is written . . ." He always did the will of God. He rebuked Peter when he counseled him not to die on the cross. He prayed, "Not my will, but thine be done," and he went to the cross to die in our place. He was not deceived, and therefore we are saved.

Everyone who trusts in Jesus Christ shall be saved. Have you trusted in him? If so, then you can rejoice, for you have a strong and sure guide to lead you every step of the way. If you have not trusted in him, I urge you to do so today. Then you too shall rejoice forever, and he shall guide you and keep you from deception.

First John 4:1 says, "Do not believe every spirit, but test the spirits to see whether they are from God, because many false prophets have gone out into the world." Ours is a spiritual as well as a material world; there are good spirits as well as bad, and we must discern between them. In Galatians 1:8 Paul says, "But even if we or an angel from heaven should preach a gospel other than the one we preached to you, let him be eternally condemned!"

The church of Ephesus refused to believe the claims of false prophets in their midst. They proved them to be frauds, and Jesus Christ commended them for their critical understanding of the gospel (Rev. 2:2). Paul speaks of such false prophets in 2 Corinthians 11:13–15: "For such men are false apostles, deceitful workmen, masquerading as apostles of Christ. And no wonder, for Satan himself masquerades as an angel of light. It is not surprising, then, if his servants masquerade as servants of righteousness. Their end will be what their actions deserve." Notice, Paul is speaking about leaders in the church. There are modern Gibeonites in the church, seeking to deceive the gullible.

Colossians 2:8 says, "See to it that no one takes you captive through hollow and deceptive philosophy, which depends on human tradition and the basic principles of this world rather than on Christ." And Ephesians 5:6 says, "Let no one deceive you with empty words." The Lord Jesus himself warns us in Matthew 24:4, "Watch out that no one deceives you."

How do we watch out? By being good students of the Scriptures, walking in the truth, and praying. We must watch and pray, lest we come into temptation. So Jesus says, "Watch out that no one deceives you. For many will come in my name, claiming, 'I am the Christ,' and will deceive many" (Matt. 24:4–5). He continues in verse 11, "And many false prophets will appear and deceive many people," and in verse 24, "For false Christs and false prophets will appear and perform great signs and miracles to deceive even the elect—if that were possible." Not only do Gibeonites present moldy bread, but they also perform signs, wonders, and miracles! Those who are naïve and gullible will be deceived if they are not careful. That is why we must watch and pray. We are to pray always in everything, we are to pray according to the word, and we are not to do anything without the Lord's direction.

First Corinthians 10:31 gives us a principle to live by: "So whether you eat or drink, or whatever you do, do it all for the glory of God." Eating and drinking refer to all activities of life. How can we do our own thing and pretend we did it for the glory of God? God receives glory only when we do what he is directing us to do. Colossians 3:17 also says: "And whatever you do, whether in word or deed, do it all in the name of the Lord Jesus, giving thanks to God the

Father through him." We are to eat, drink, speak, and act, all for God's glory, by his authority, and in accordance with his revelation, so that we can give thanks to God.

Every aspect of our life should be lived for the glory of God; no part is exempt! This is what the confession "Jesus is Lord" means. If the mighty Joshua could be deceived and yield to temptation, so can we. Therefore, we must not do anything without first earnestly inquiring of the Lord and receiving guidance from him. James Boice quotes the following counsel from Alan Redpath:

> Never, never, NEVER trust your own judgment in anything. When common sense says that a course is right, lift your heart to God, for the path of faith and the path of blessing may be in a direction completely opposite to that which you call common sense. When voices tell you that action is urgent, that something must be done immediately, refer everything to the tribunal of heaven. Then, if you are still in doubt, dare to stand still. If you are called on to act and you have not time to pray, don't act. If you are called on to move in a certain direction and cannot wait until you have peace with God about it, don't move. Be strong enough and brave enough to dare to stand and wait on God, for none of them who wait on him shall ever be ashamed. That is the only way to outmatch the devil. (Joshua: We Will Serve the Lord, 99–100)

Wrong decisions have disastrous consequences, both for this life and for the generations to come. The Bible says, "Do not be deceived: God cannot be mocked. A man reaps what he sows" (Gal. 6:7). Our wrong decisions affect not only us, but all who are under our leadership—our spouse, our children, our congregation—and it goes on for generations. Look at the wrong decision made by Adam and Eve, and its disastrous consequences for all mankind. Look at the wrong decision of David in the case of Bathsheba—the sword did not depart from his house. Remember the foolish decision of Lot, who chose for himself grass and brought tragedy upon himself and all his descendants. Joshua's wrong decision brought about murmuring and disunity for the first time in that generation of Israel, and introduced a foreign people into the community to be a constant source of temptation.

How to Make Wise Decisions

How, then, can we make wise decisions?

1. Be an earnest student of the Scriptures and steep yourself in God's truth.
2. Pray earnestly to hear God's will. In everything—for big things and small things—pray. Do not pray, "Let Ishmael live" (Gen. 17:18). God is not here to stamp his approval on our subjective desires. Be willing to hear even the exact opposite of what you want to do.
3. Oppose all schemes of modern Gibeonites, and do so by the Spirit of God. Reject antinomianism and subjectivism.
4. Reject "feel-good" preaching that entertains and soothes, but will never save.
5. Reject the false "signs and wonders" ministries of modern Gibeonites that are designed to deceive the gullible.
6. Reject health, wealth, and political power theology. It will never get you to heaven.
7. Reject the idea that singing hymns and choruses can replace the preaching of God's word. The sermon should be the centerpiece of the worship service.
8. Do not fellowship with Christians who have no desire to walk in the way of obedience. What fellowship has Christ with Belial?
9. Do not uncritically trust media and advertisements, including Christian ones. They are there to beguile

you. Do not listen to questionable music, even if it is labeled "Christian."

10. Do not make decisions, especially in the following matters, without earnest inquiry of the Lord:

    a. Education.

    b. Marriage. This is a serious issue. Suppose you are interested in two people—one is good-looking, the other just average. But the difference is that one has nothing to do with God and the other loves God. If you trust in appearances, you will make a wrong decision, which can have disastrous consequences.

    c. Career. Pray earnestly about what job to accept and what offers to turn down.

    d. Church membership. What church should you be a member of? Do not be deceived by Gibeonites. You should choose a church that is committed to preaching the Scriptures, administers the sacraments properly, and exercises discipline. When people come to church seeking membership, leaders should examine them carefully to see whether they are serious about walking with Christ. Finally, if you get a feeling that you want to leave your church, pray and seek the Lord, because that decision will be destructive if you do it for your own reasons.

    e. Expenditures of time and money. You and I have no freedom to spend our time and money any way we want. It is the Lord's time and money; we must be directed by God so we can spend these for his glory and in his name.

    f. Where to live. Ask God where he wants you to live. The American spirit is to live for a while in one place, then pack up and move to another, and then to yet another—usually to make more money. It may have nothing to do with God's plan for our lives.

Brothers and sisters, we must strive to make correct decisions. The only way to do this is to seek wisdom from above. Pray earnestly and continually that you will not be deceived. This is especially important for leaders, because when you fail, you affect many people. Follow the example of our Lord Jesus Christ, who always did the will of his Father, not his own will. Do all things for the glory of God and in the name of God, and the promise of Proverbs 3:5–6 will be yours: "Trust in the LORD with all your heart and lean not on your own understanding; in all your ways acknowledge him, and he will make your paths straight."

10

When God Laughs, Watch Out!

Joshua 10–12

The Lord said to Joshua, "Do not be afraid of them; I have given them into your hand. Not one of them will be able to withstand you."

Joshua 10:8

Chapters 10 through 12 of Joshua begin the account of Israel's conquest of Canaan in compliance with the expressed command of God. The divine judgment received by the Canaanite nations foreshadows the final day of judgment, when each of us must give an account to the living God, the Judge of all the earth. The Judge is none other than Jesus Christ, the eternal Son (John 5:22, 28–30). The doctrine of judgment taught in Joshua thus has great relevance for us today, and we are wise if we heed its warning.

God, the Judge of All Men

Modern day preachers largely ignore the doctrine of divine judgment; they prefer to present God as a kind, grandfatherly figure who is never angry with anyone. In doing this, they have moved away from historic, orthodox Christianity. By contrast, the seventeenth-century Westminster Confession of Faith devotes serious attention to this biblical doctrine in chapter 33, "Of the Last Judgment":

> Section 1: God hath appointed a day, wherein He will judge the world in righteousness by Jesus Christ, to whom all power and judgment is given of the Father. In which day, not only the apostate angels shall be judged, but likewise all persons that have lived upon earth shall appear before the tribunal of Christ, to give an account of their thoughts, words, and deeds; and to receive according to what they have done in the body, whether good or evil.

> Section 2: The end of God's appointing this day is for the manifestation of the glory of His mercy, in the eternal salvation of the elect; and of His justice, in the damnation of the reprobate, who are wicked and disobedient. For then shall the righteous go into everlasting life, and receive that fullness of joy and refreshing, which shall come from the presence of the Lord; but the wicked who know not God, and obey not the Gospel of Jesus Christ, shall be cast into eternal torments, and be punished with everlasting destruction from the presence of the Lord, and from the glory of His power.

> Section 3: As Christ would have us to be certainly persuaded that there shall be a day of judgment, both to deter all men from sin; and for the greater consolation of the godly in their adversity: so will He have that day unknown to men, that they may shake off all carnal security, and be always watchful, because they know not at what hour the Lord will come; and may be ever prepared to say, Come Lord Jesus, come quickly, Amen.

Our God is a moral God; he is light and in him there is no darkness at all. This moral God punishes sin in history and beyond history. The flood described in Genesis 7 wiped out all but eight people. Later, God patiently endured the wickedness of the Canaanites for four hundred years, but they showed "contempt for the riches of his kindness, tolerance and patience, not realizing that God's kindness leads . . . toward repentance" (Rom. 2:4). Their continued lack of repentance eventually brought God's judgment upon them. God instructed Moses and Joshua not to show mercy to the Canaanites, but to destroy them all—men, women, and children (Deut. 7 and 20).

We do not like to hear about such destruction because we have been influenced by the modern view of Jesus. We have reduced Jesus Christ, the Lord of the universe, to one who loves and forgives everybody. But it was God himself who commanded Joshua to destroy all the Canaanites. We must have a proper biblical understanding of God. He is both the Savior and the Sovereign Judge. Romans 11:22 says, "Behold therefore the goodness and severity of God: on them which fell, severity; but toward thee, goodness, if thou continue in his goodness: otherwise, thou also shalt be cut off" (KJV).

God has appointed every man once to die and then face judgment (Heb. 9:27). In light of this reality, we must understand that today is the day of grace, the day of salvation, the day of God's kindness. God wants us to repent and turn to Jesus Christ, that we may be saved from his coming wrath. Everyone who persists in wickedness and rebellion will face an angry, just Judge. "He will punish those who do not know God and do not obey the gospel of our Lord Jesus. They will be punished with everlasting destruction and shut out from the presence of the Lord and from the majesty of his power" (2 Thess. 1:8–9).

God is not at all intimidated by those who rebel against him; in fact, he laughs at the rebellious before he pours out his wrath upon them. Psalm 2 says, "Why do the nations conspire and the peoples plot in vain? The kings of the earth take their stand and the rulers gather together against the LORD and against his Anointed One. 'Let us break their chains,' they say, 'and throw off their fetters'" (vv. 1–3). These people see the law of God as a chain that binds them, and they desire to be free from his rule. But verse 4 tells us, "The One enthroned in heaven laughs; the Lord scoffs at them. Then he rebukes them in his anger and terrifies them in his wrath." The psalm concludes with a solemn warning to those who would rebel against the Judge of all the earth: "Therefore, you kings, be wise; be warned, you rulers of the earth. Serve the LORD with fear and rejoice with trembling. Kiss the Son, lest he be angry and you be destroyed in your way, for his wrath can flare up in a moment. Blessed are all who take refuge in him" (vv. 10–12). When God laughs, watch out!

The Canaanite Kings Conspire

The Canaanites knew of the advance of the kingdom of God in power: "Now Adoni-Zedek king of Jerusalem heard that Joshua had taken Ai and totally destroyed it" (Josh. 10:1). They also knew that the Gibeonites had surrendered and found mercy. The northern and southern confederacies were well aware of these events, yet they refused to capitulate. Instead, the five southern kings, led by Adoni-Zedek king of Jerusalem, decided to attack the Gibeonites (10:3–5), while the northern kings, under the leadership of Jabin king of Hazor, went up against Israel (11:1–5). They stubbornly refused to surrender and sue for peace. They refused to call themselves servants of Joshua, as the Gibeonites had done. They refused to entreat him, saying, "Have mercy upon us! We are sinners." This is still true today. When people hear the gospel preached and are told that the kingdom of God is at hand, the vast majority of them refuse to believe.

The Canaanites hardened their hearts and the Lord confirmed them in their stubbornness. "Except for the

Hivites living in Gibeon, not one city made a treaty of peace with the Israelites, who took them all in battle. For it was the LORD himself who hardened their hearts to wage war against Israel, so that he might destroy them totally, exterminating them without mercy, as the LORD had commanded Moses" (Josh. 11:19–20). It is sobering to realize that when a person hardens his heart, refusing to repent and accept God's gracious offer of peace, God continues the process until that person is destroyed. Pharaoh hardened his heart, and he was destroyed. Indeed, all those who have hardened their hearts throughout history have perished. We must examine our own response to the word of God. Do we repent and believe, or do our hearts remain hard?

The Canaanite Kings Hanged

Although these kings conspired together to oppose the Lord, he was not alarmed; he merely laughed at them. "The LORD said to Joshua, 'Do not be afraid of them; I have given them into your hand. Not one of them will be able to withstand you'" (Josh. 10:8). God is not afraid of anyone, for he is the Sovereign Lord. He opposes every arrogant person. In Joshua 11:6 God told Joshua again, "Do not be afraid of them, because by this time tomorrow I will hand all of them over to Israel, slain. You are to hamstring their horses and burn their chariots."

Joshua 10:11 tells us what happened to some of these defiant Canaanites: "As they fled before Israel on the road down from Beth Horon to Azekah, the LORD hurled large hailstones down on them from the sky, and more of them died from the hailstones than were killed by the swords of the Israelites." Oh, the severity of God! As the hailstones fell, the five arrogant kings of the southern coalition ran for their lives. They hid in a cave in Makkedah, thinking they could hide from God. What nonsense! God knows all things; everything is laid bare before him. The psalmist rightly asked, "Where can I flee from your presence?" (Ps. 139:7). There is no place in the universe where we can hide from God.

Joshua brought the kings out and made them lie down on the ground. Then he called the Israelite leaders and said, "Come here and put your feet on the necks of these kings" (10:24). Joshua killed these men who had thought they could defeat God, and he hung their dead bodies on trees as an evidence of their having been under God's curse (Deut. 21:23).

Joshua 10:28 continues, "That day Joshua took Makkedah. He put the city and its king to the sword and totally destroyed everyone in it. He left no survivors." This is exactly what God had commanded in Deuteronomy 7 and 20. Never make light of the severity of God! When one refuses to repent and believe on the Lord Jesus Christ, he makes himself a candidate to experience such judgment.

Joshua then proceeded to destroy Libnah, Lachish, Eglon, Hebron, and Debir. He conquered the entire southern region in a single campaign (10:29–42). What about the northern coalition? "Joshua took all these royal cities and their kings and put them to the sword. He totally destroyed them" (11:12). And what about Hazor, the most important city in Canaan? "At that time Joshua turned back and captured Hazor and put its king to the sword. (Hazor had been the head of all these kingdoms.) Everyone in it they put to the sword. They totally destroyed them, not sparing anything that breathed" (11:10–11). The Israelites then burned Hazor, as they had done to Jericho and Ai.

Finally, what about the Anakim, the tall, strong people who had frightened the spies forty years earlier? "At that time Joshua went and destroyed the Anakites from the hill country: from Hebron, Debir and Anab, from all the hill country of Judah, and from all the hill country of

Israel. Joshua totally destroyed them and their towns. No Anakites were left in Israelite territory" (11:21–22). God's sure judgment fell on every unrepentant Canaanite. Not one of God's enemies prevailed.

The Lord Himself Hanged Them

It was the Lord who destroyed these people and hanged these kings. Joshua and Israel did not go on a rampage and kill innocent men and women. No, the Lord himself executed judgment on the Canaanites after they persisted in living in sin for four hundred years. He has both the right and the might to judge. We need to ask again: Have we sufficiently appreciated the truth that Jesus is Lord? Lord means sovereign—he has all authority in heaven and on earth to do what he pleases.

Joshua 10 highlights God's role in defeating Israel's enemies: "The LORD threw them into confusion" (v. 10), "The LORD gave the Amorites over to Israel" (v. 12), "The LORD your God has given them into your hand" (v. 19), "The LORD handed Lachish over to Israel" (v. 32), and "All these kings and their lands Joshua conquered . . . because the LORD, the God of Israel, fought for Israel" (v. 42). The Lord himself did this—the infinite, personal, self-existing, self-sufficient, almighty covenant God. He was the primary actor in Israel's battles. He is the sovereign One; he does what he pleases, and all that he does is just. He receives glory in both his judgment and his salvation. All who defy him will experience his severity both here and hereafter.

The entire Bible presents God as a mighty warrior. After the Lord defeated the Egyptian army, Moses and the Israelites declared, "The LORD is a warrior; the LORD is his name" (Exod. 15:3). As well, the Old Testament priests encouraged the soldiers going into battle by saying, "Do not be terrified . . . for the LORD your God is the one who goes with you to fight for you against your enemies to give you victory" (Deut. 20:3–4).

The Lord never changes; he is immutable. The Lord of the Old Testament is the Lord of the New Testament. In the book of Revelation, John gives us a clear picture of who this Lord Jesus is, and what the future holds for those who oppose him:

> I saw heaven standing open and there before me was a white horse, whose rider is called Faithful and True. With justice he judges and makes war. His eyes are like blazing fire, and on his head are many crowns. He has a name written on him that no one knows but he himself. He is dressed in a robe dipped in blood, and his name is the Word of God. The armies of heaven were following him, riding on white horses and dressed in fine linen, white and clean. Out of his mouth comes a sharp sword with which to strike down the nations. "He will rule them with an iron scepter." He treads the winepress of the fury of the wrath of God Almighty. On his robe and on his thigh he has this name written: KING OF KINGS AND LORD OF LORDS. (Rev. 19:11–16)

Modern Christians do not like to think of Jesus as one who wages war against his enemies. We prefer to think of him as a meek and gentle Savior, but he is depicted here as a warrior king with an iron scepter. And what is he doing? Meting out the wrath of God.

John continues, "And I saw an angel standing in the sun, who cried in a loud voice to all the birds flying in midair, 'Come, gather together for the great supper of God, so that you may eat the flesh of kings, generals, and mighty men, of horses and their riders, and the flesh of all people, free and slave, small and great'" (Rev. 19:17–18). God's total victory over his enemies is what we find in Joshua 10–12. These chapters thus foreshadow the final triumph of our Lord Jesus Christ.

All judgment has been given to Jesus Christ. The resurrection of Christ is the proof that God is going to judge us by this One whom he raised from the dead (Acts 17:31). Jesus Christ alone is Judge, and he is going to judge all people everywhere. This "will take place on the day when God will judge men's secrets through Jesus Christ" (Rom. 2:16). He knows everything that we have thought, said, and done. We can keep no secrets from him. In Revelation 20 we read:

> Then I saw a great white throne and him who was seated on it. Earth and sky fled from his presence, and there was no place for them. And I saw the dead, great and small, standing before the throne, and books were opened. Another book was opened, which is the book of life. The dead were judged according to what they had done as recorded in the books. The sea gave up the dead that were in it, and death and Hades gave up the dead that were in them, and each person was judged according to what he had done. Then death and Hades were thrown into the lake of fire. The lake of fire is the second death. If anyone's name was not found written in the book of life, he was thrown into the lake of fire. (vv. 11–15)

See the severity of God! The lake of fire is empty now, but the time is coming when it will be filled. It is designed for the devil and his angels, as well as for every person who served the devil rather than Jesus Christ.

The Lord Himself Was Hanged

We have seen how the Lord himself hanged the Canaanite kings, but that is not the end of the story. Another one was also hanged. The incarnate Son of God, the Lord Jesus Christ, who never committed any sin, was killed and hanged on a tree. What is the meaning of his death?

Jesus Christ was the suffering servant who was obedient even to the death of the cross. He became incarnate in order to die for our sins. He who knew no sin died the

105

accursed death that belonged to us. We are the lawless ones who deserve to die, as stated in Deuteronomy 27:26: "Cursed is the man who does not uphold the words of this law by carrying them out." Yet God, in great love and mercy, did not spare his Son. Jesus Christ died on the cross for our salvation, to spare us from eternal damnation and the lake of fire. "Christ redeemed us from the curse of the law by becoming a curse for us" (Gal. 3:13).

Christ's death was a triumph, for by it he destroyed death and all enemies. "Having disarmed the powers and authorities, he made a public spectacle of them, triumphing over them by the cross" (Col. 2:15). Christ is the risen and victorious Lord. He is the Savior and the Judge. Everything is placed under his feet.

Our Responsibilities

What, then, are our responsibilities?

1. *We ourselves must repent and believe on the Lord Jesus Christ and be saved.* If you have not done that, I urge you to do so today. If you have never feared this Christ, do so now. Fall down before him and surrender to him. "Kiss the Son, lest he be angry . . . for his wrath can flare up in a moment" (Ps. 2:12). If you remain a hardened rebel, rejecting the gospel and refusing to repent, you will be placed under the feet of Jesus Christ, and he will, in due time, mete out judgment.

2. *We must proclaim the gospel.* Joshua was charged to destroy God's enemies, but we are charged to proclaim the gospel and urge them to be saved. We must tell them, "Repent, for the kingdom of God is at hand. Now is the accepted time, now is the day of salvation. Surrender to the Lord Jesus Christ and be safe from his wrath. The King has come to save, but if you harden your heart against the Sovereign Lord Jesus, you will be judged by him." Through the gospel, God commands

all people everywhere to repent and seek refuge in Jesus. We must speak about repentance, for there is no salvation without it. As Jesus himself did, we are to tell people, "Repent or perish" (Luke 13:3). Everyone who calls upon the name of the Lord, as Rahab and the Gibeonites did, will be saved.

3. *We must put to death any known sin in us.* We are not to feed sin; we are to kill it! "Everyone who confesses the name of the Lord must turn away from wickedness" (2 Tim. 2:19). We have a responsibility to live holy lives worthy of our heavenly calling by mortifying daily the evil that is within us. We do so by the power of the Holy Spirit. Paul reminds us that sin still dwells in us: "For the sinful nature desires what is contrary to the Spirit, and the Spirit what is contrary to the sinful nature. They are in conflict with each other" (Gal. 5:17). There is a conflict within us, so we have to wage war. "For if you live according to the sinful nature, you will die; but if by the Spirit you put to death the misdeeds of the body, you will live" (Rom. 8:13). We must fight sin until the day we die. The modern view that someone can continue in sin and be saved is false. God commands us, "Be holy, because I am holy" (1 Pet. 1:16). Anything else is a doctrine of demons.

When we think about what awaits us when Christ comes again, it should cause us to tremble.

> God is just: He will pay back trouble to those who trouble you and give relief to you who are troubled, and to us as well. This will happen when the Lord Jesus is revealed from heaven in blazing fire with his powerful angels. He will punish those who do not know God and do not obey the gospel of our Lord Jesus. They will be punished with everlasting destruction and shut out from the presence of the Lord and from the majesty of his power on the day he comes to be glorified in his holy people and to be marveled at among all those who have believed. This includes you, because you believed our testimony to you. (2 Thess. 1:6–10)

Do you fear God enough to forsake your sin and respond to him in obedience? Consider the kindness and the severity of God—severity to those who rebel, but kindness to us who joyfully embrace his beneficent rule.

11

The Faith of Caleb

Joshua 14

So Hebron has belonged to Caleb son of Jephunneh the Kenizzite ever since, because he followed the LORD, the God of Israel, wholeheartedly.

Joshua 14:14

The hallmark of genuine Christianity is faith, for without faith it is impossible to please God (Heb. 11:6). As Christians grow older, they should grow in faith. The classic example of vital, persevering faith is that of Caleb ben-Jephunneh. Joshua 14 focuses on Caleb, a man who pleased God and obeyed him fully. Still a strong warrior at eighty-five years of age, he personally defeated the ancient race of giants who dwelt in Hebron. Commended by God for his perseverance, Caleb is an inspiration to all true believers; therefore, let us examine the various aspects of Caleb's mighty faith.

Faith Waits

By faith, Caleb waited patiently on the Lord. Born in Egypt, Caleb began life much like any one of his fellow Hebrews. He lived the first thirty-eight years of his life as a slave of Pharaoh and was subjected to hard labor. Yet Caleb believed God and his promises. He added faith to the word he heard through Moses that God would soon bring about deliverance for his people (Exod. 4:29–31).

All of Caleb's generation saw God's extraordinary miracles in Egypt, at the Red Sea, and in the wilderness; but Caleb was one of the few who added faith to what he heard and saw. When others murmured at Marah, Caleb trusted God. When many worshiped the golden calf, Caleb remained faithful to Yahweh. As a result, God himself bore witness concerning Caleb's character, saying, "Caleb has a different spirit and follows me wholeheartedly" (Num. 14:24). Not only did the Lord commend him, but he also promised that Caleb would inherit the city of Hebron in the hill country (Josh. 14:9–13). And throughout the intervening years, Caleb by faith kept this promise in mind. Nothing could shatter his conviction that one day he would conquer Hebron and live in it. He had to wait patiently—at least forty-five years—to receive the fulfillment of God's promise, but Caleb persevered by faith.

Faith Leads

Being a man of great faith, Caleb became one of the leaders of Judah. He remained faithful to the Lord when most of the Israelites became guilty of disobedience and unbelief. In Numbers 13:6 we read that he was one of the twelve leaders of Israel chosen to spy out the land of Canaan. Unlike the majority of his fellow spies, he encouraged the people to trust in God for victory over the Canaanite inhabitants (Num. 14:6–9). Later he was named by the Lord to assist Moses in assigning the land as the inheritance of the twelve tribes (Num. 34:16–19). Finally, we see Caleb leading the men of Judah in conquering Hebron and the other cities in the hill country (Judg. 1:9–11; Josh. 15:13–15). Caleb led both by faith and by example.

Faith Speaks

Active faith speaks God's word. When ten of the spies discouraged Israel from obeying God's word to go in and take possession of Canaan by conquest, Caleb and Joshua spoke for God. The ten unbelieving spies declared that the people of Canaan were giants and that the Israelites should go back to Egypt. Caleb, however, declared in faith, "The covenant Lord, the infinite personal God, the God of miracles who delivered us from Egypt, is pleased with us. He will lead us into the land. He will fight for us and give the land to us. Only do not be afraid." An unbeliever sees only giants; a true believer also sees God.

In 2 Corinthians 4:13 the apostle Paul says, "It is written: 'I believed; therefore I have spoken.' With that same spirit of faith we also believe and therefore speak." When we believe God's promises, we will speak for God as Caleb did. What about you? Do you believe God? Do you speak of his power to save us, guide us, and fight our battles? We should all emulate faithful Caleb.

Faith Claims God's Promises

True faith cannot be discouraged, because its confidence rests in God's word. As Caleb grew older, his faith remained focused on the specific promises he had received from the Lord forty-five years earlier. As the Israelites crossed the Jordan, fought their battles, and conquered the land, mighty Caleb fought alongside the younger soldiers. Now, after seven years of warfare, the time came to divide the land among the various tribes. When Judah's turn came, the people moved forward. But before their portion could be assigned,

Caleb stepped up and told Joshua, "Wait! You cannot assign Hebron to anyone else. I have a claim to it. God promised it to me forty-five years ago."

What was the heart of Caleb's argument? "The Lord promised." Caleb was telling Joshua, "You don't need to cast lots or pray. God has already revealed his will in this matter. Hebron is mine!" Notice Caleb's emphasis on the word of the Lord as he made his case before Joshua:

> You know what the LORD said to Moses the man of God at Kadesh Barnea about you and me. I was forty years old when Moses the servant of the LORD sent me from Kadesh Barnea to explore the land. And I brought him back a report according to my convictions. . . . So on that day Moses swore to me, "The land on which your feet have walked will be your inheritance and that of your children forever, because you have followed the LORD my God wholeheartedly." Now then, just as the LORD promised, he has kept me alive for forty-five years since the time he said this to Moses. (Josh. 14:6–10)

Joshua could not deny Caleb's petition, for it was based on the Lord and his promise. So Joshua blessed Caleb and gave him his portion.

The basis of Caleb's petition was the promise of God. This ought to be the basis of our prayers as well: "Lord, you have promised; now do it for me." This is how David prayed in 2 Samuel 7:25: "And now, LORD God, keep forever the promise you have made concerning your servant and his house. Do as you promised." What a mighty argument! This is the essence of powerful, prevailing prayer. We should pray according to the will of God, according to what God has promised. Every promise in the Bible is ours.

Faith Fights

Faith not only claims but also fights for what has been promised. Caleb was willing to fight for his inheritance;

he was not one to flee from the prospect of battle. He was not a covenant-breaker or a quitter; as troubles came, he grew stronger, bolder, and more confident in God.

God had preserved Caleb so that, even though he was now eighty-five years old, he was still physically and spiritually vigorous. When others would have retired to pursue quieter interests, Caleb was ready for war. At that time, Hebron was occupied by a race of giants, about thirteen feet tall. But Caleb was not afraid. He gloried in the opportunity to defeat these enemies of God. He was not, however, self-confident; rather, he declared, "The LORD helping me, I will drive them out" (Josh. 14:12). That is the secret of every believer's success. Caleb demonstrated the truth later penned by the apostle Paul, "I can do everything through him who gives me strength" (Phil. 4:13). We also should be fighters—unafraid, confident, and unshakable in God. We must declare with Caleb, "The Lord helping me, I will drive out the giants from my inheritance."

Faith Obeys

Genuine faith obeys God's commands. The Bible declares six times that Caleb obeyed the Lord fully—a unique commendation. How many "Christians" today say, "Because we are saved, we don't have to obey"! Such declarations are in fact proof that they are not God's people. True believers are "God's workmanship, created in Christ Jesus to do good works, which God prepared in advance for us to do" (Eph. 2:10). Obedience to the covenant Lord is proof of our love for him. How can anyone call Jesus "Lord" and not do his will?

False believers may call Jesus "Lord," but they refuse to obey him. Not so Caleb. God himself certified that Caleb was fully obedient to him, saying, "My servant Caleb has a different spirit and follows me wholeheartedly"

(Num. 14:24). Yet we must understand that Caleb was not sinless. Only Jesus is sinless; no one else can ever be sinless in this life. But we must never use our fallen nature as an excuse to walk in disobedience. Caleb's life proves that full, wholehearted obedience is the norm for the Christian life, not an unachievable ideal.

God calls us "my servant" and is pleased when we fully obey him as Caleb did, not turning aside to the right or to the left. That is what it means to be led by the Spirit. The Bible says that those who are led by the Spirit are alone the sons of God (Rom. 8:14). We who are regenerate enjoy the freedom of *posse non peccare*, the freedom not to sin, because we have a new nature, we have the Holy Spirit within us, and we have God's revelation to tell us the way to live.

Faith Conquers

Finally, genuine faith perseveres and ultimately conquers. Scripture documents Caleb's success: "From Hebron Caleb drove out the three Anakites—Sheshai, Ahiman, and Talmai—descendants of Anak" (Josh. 15:14), and "As Moses had promised, Hebron was given to Caleb, who drove from it the three sons of Anak" (Judg. 1:20). Caleb's faith was bold, conquering faith. Earlier he had been persecuted for this faith and had nearly been stoned (Num. 14:10). Then he had to patiently endure forty-five years in the desert, suffering for the sins of the community. But faith does not give up; rather, it waits patiently to see God fulfill his promises. Faith knows that the almighty, immutable God does not lie, and that "no matter how many promises God has made, they are 'Yes' in Christ" (2 Cor. 1:20). Therefore, faith waits and faith wins!

Caleb defeated the giants in the name of the Lord because God was with him. But the book of Judges tells us that other Israelites failed: "Manasseh did not drive out the people of Beth Shan or Taanach or Dor or Ibleam or Megiddo and their surrounding settlements . . . nor did Ephraim drive out the Canaanites living in Gezer . . . neither did Zebulun drive out the Canaanites living in Kitron or Nahalol . . . nor did Asher drive out those living in Acco or Sidon or Ahlab or Aczib or Helbah or Aphek or Rehob . . . neither did Naphtali drive out those living in Beth Shemesh or Beth Anath" (Judg. 1:27–33). Why were they unable to drive these Canaanites out? Unbelief. They did not have faith in God's promise and they therefore did not put up a fight.

That may be true of some of us as well. Are you living a defeated life? Have you grown accustomed to failure? Let me assure you, that is not God's purpose for you. God's will is that we live victorious Christian lives, but if we do not believe his promises, we too will fail to enjoy our inheritance.

Our Inheritance

Caleb and his descendants rested in Hebron, the land of his inheritance. The name "Hebron" means communion and fellowship with God. It is the very place where Abraham built an altar and worshiped God (Gen. 13:18). Real estate, however, is not the primary inheritance to which Christians look forward. The Scriptures direct our hopes elsewhere. The psalmist declares, "Whom have I in heaven but you? And earth has nothing I desire besides you. My flesh and my heart may fail, but God is the strength of my heart and my portion forever" (Ps. 73:25–26). Jeremiah likewise speaks of his divine inheritance: "'The LORD is my portion; therefore I will wait for him.' The LORD is good to those whose hope is in him, to the one who seeks him; it is good to wait quietly for the salvation of the LORD" (Lam. 3:24–26).

We find our rest in God alone. Let me ask you: Is the Lord your portion? Is he your treasure? If so, then you will love him with all your heart and keep his commands as Caleb did. That is precisely how Jesus describes true rest: "Whoever has my commands and obeys them, he is the one who loves me. He who loves me will be loved by my Father, and I too will love him and show myself to him" (John 14:21). This is what a true believer is excited about—that communion, that Hebron, that fellowship with God. We cannot enjoy this communion, however, without obedience. Jesus continues, "If anyone loves me, he will obey my teaching. My Father will love him, and we will come to him and make our home with him" (v. 23). We are delighted, nourished, and invigorated through fellowship with God. We do not need real estate, fame, or power in this world; rather, we seek the kingdom of God and God himself. Nothing else can make us happy.

Whether you are young or old, learn from Caleb and follow his example. Be faithful to the covenant Lord, and trust in his promises. Do not seek ease, but fight the Lord's battles in the Lord's might. Only then will our testimony echo that of the psalmist: "The righteous will flourish like a palm tree, they will grow like a cedar of Lebanon; planted in the house of the LORD, they will flourish in the courts of our God. They will still bear fruit in old age, they will stay fresh and green, proclaiming, 'The LORD is upright; he is my Rock, and there is no wickedness in him'" (Ps. 92:12–15).

12

Escaping the Death Penalty

Joshua 20

Then the LORD said to Joshua: "Tell the Israelites to designate the cities of refuge, as I instructed you through Moses, so that anyone who kills a person accidentally and unintentionally may flee there and find protection from the avenger of blood."

Joshua 20:1–3

What does the Bible teach about the death penalty? Many who speak about the sanctity of all life oppose capital punishment. Although we agree with such people in their strong opposition to abortion, we disagree with their opposition to capital punishment. The death penalty for a capital offense is thoroughly scriptural, and Christians are to submit to the authority of Scripture in every matter.

We will consider, first, what the Scripture says about capital punishment, especially for the crime of murder; then we will consider the cities of refuge that

God instituted to show mercy to those who murdered someone unintentionally; finally, we will speak about Jesus Christ, who is the true city of refuge for all sinners who flee to him.

Capital Punishment

Genesis 9:6 records the first reference to the death penalty for the crime of murder: "Whoever sheds the blood of man, by man shall his blood be shed; for in the image of God has God made man." Here God declares that a murderer deserves death because he has killed one who is made in the image of God. Being the image-bearer of God does not mean that man is God, but that man is like God, especially in his moral qualities and rationality. Contrary to the claims of some, man is not a mere animal. Therefore, the act of murdering a man is an assault on the honor of God, and the murderer must be put to death.

The death penalty for murder is not abrogated in the New Testament. God explicitly gives the state authority to exercise the power of the sword:

> Everyone must submit himself to the governing authorities, for there is no authority except that which God has established. The authorities that exist have been established by God. Consequently, he who rebels against the authority is rebelling against what God has instituted, and those who do so will bring judgment on themselves. For rulers hold no terror for those who do right, but for those who do wrong. Do you want to be free from fear of the one in authority? Then do what is right and he will commend you. For he is God's servant to do you good. But if you do wrong, be afraid, for he does not bear the sword for nothing. He is God's servant, an agent of wrath to bring punishment on the wrongdoer. Therefore, it is necessary to submit to the authorities, not only because of possible punishment but also because of conscience. (Rom. 13:1–5)

Three times in this passage we are told that the state is granted authority by God himself. We are also told three times that the state is a minister of God, and that its function is to punish evil and promote good. To this end, God gives the state the power of the sword, which is capital punishment. Interestingly, Paul wrote this not about a Christian state but about the pagan Roman government of his time.

Scripture never speaks about reforming a murderer. That is a modern idea. Instead, God requires the state to mete out capital punishment to murderers, thus upholding both the sanctity of life and the justice and honor of God.

The Cities of Refuge

Individual blood vengeance was widespread in the Near East before the formation of the people of Israel. The avenger of blood, the nearest male relative of the victim, had a duty to pursue the murderer and kill him, and he did not differentiate between intentional and unintentional killing. God himself demanded vengeance for a deliberate act of murder, but he also made provision for sparing the life of one who killed a person accidentally, without premeditation. Thus God required Israel to set apart six cities of refuge, three on the east side of the Jordan River and three on the west, to which one who unintentionally killed another could flee and be safe from the avenger of blood (Exod. 21:12–14; Num. 35:6–34; Deut. 4:41–43, 19:113; Josh. 20:19).

These cities were to be centrally located and built on eminent locations so they could be easily seen and reached by all. Their gates were to be kept unlocked. God told Moses to build roads so that people could reach them safely; periodically, the roads were to be cleared of all debris so that nothing would hinder a person in his flight.

Additionally, large signs with directions to the cities were to be posted at all crossroads. Not only Israelites, but also aliens were permitted to flee to these cities.

The person escaping individual blood vengeance had to submit to God's specific protocol. When he reached the city, he had to stop at the gates and present his case to the court of elders at the gate. After a preliminary hearing, he would be given conditional asylum. Then the authorities had to establish the circumstances of the killing. If the killing was proven by the testimonies of two or more witnesses to be unintentional, the refugee was permitted to stay in the city until the death of the high priest. He would then be free to return to his own city and family without fear of molestation. If the assembly determined, however, that the murderer had indeed killed someone intentionally, he would be handed over to the avenger of blood to be executed. Thus the land would be cleansed of any defilement.

Christ, Our True Refuge

The cities of refuge were established by divine initiative and mercy, but only those who were truly innocent were spared from death. These cities point to the Lord Jesus Christ, who is the true city of refuge to which every sinner can flee and be saved from eternal death. All can find refuge in him—not only those who have sinned unintentionally, but also those who have sinned intentionally.

King David found this type of refuge after he committed a capital offense. We are told that he deliberately killed Uriah the Hittite, a godly Gentile convert: "In the morning David wrote a letter to Joab and sent it with Uriah. In it he wrote, 'Put Uriah in the front line where the fighting is fiercest. Then withdraw from him so he will be struck down and die'" (2 Sam. 11:14–15). Later, the prophet Nathan confronted David: "Why did you despise the word of the LORD by doing what is evil in his eyes? You struck down Uriah the Hittite with the sword and took his wife to be your own. You killed him with the sword of the Ammonites" (2 Sam. 12:9). It is clear that David murdered Uriah intentionally, yet in Psalm 51 we find him asking God to forgive his sins: "Save me from bloodguilt, O God, the God who saves me, and my tongue will sing of your righteousness" (v. 14). David found refuge in the Lord Jesus Christ.

The truth is, while we may not all be murderers, we are all guilty of sin. The Bible emphatically declares, "There is no one righteous, . . . no one who understands, no one who seeks God, . . . no one who does good, not even one. . . . All have sinned and fall short of the glory of God" (Rom. 3:10–12, 23). We all are born sinners and we practice sin daily. Consequently, all of us are guilty and under the sentence of death—not only physical death, but, more importantly, eternal death (Rom. 6:23).

Is there a city of refuge to which such wicked people can flee and be safe? Or to put it more bluntly, does God justify the wicked? Thanks be to God, the gospel tells us that he does: "To the man who does not work but trusts God who justifies the wicked, his faith is credited as righteousness" (Rom. 4:5). That is why the gospel is called good news. "The wages of sin is death, but the gift of God is eternal life in Christ Jesus our Lord" (Rom. 6:23). David the murderer fled to Christ, where his sins were forgiven and he was saved from the penalty of eternal death. We too must flee to Jesus for refuge!

In Jesus our sins can be forgiven. But how can this be? Is God not just? Yes, he is just, but Jesus satisfied his justice by suffering God's death penalty in our behalf. The eternal Son of God became incarnate that he might die on the cross in our place. His death counted as our death, the death we deserve for our sins. "God made him who had no sin to be sin for us, so that in him we might become the righteousness of God" (2 Cor. 5:21). But we must run to him and trust in him in order to be safe from the divine justice and death that pursues us. Jesus Christ died in the place of every sinner who repents and believes on him.

The cities of refuge in ancient Israel were thus a type of refuge from wrath; Jesus Christ is the genuine city of refuge for all who have sinned, whether intentionally or unintentionally. Just as in the days of old, this refuge is centrally located; as the Scripture says, "The word is near you; it is in your mouth and in your heart" (Deut. 30:14; Rom. 10:8). The way to this refuge is also clearly marked, both in the written Scriptures and whenever the gospel is proclaimed. The Christian's duty is to make Jesus known by speaking about his incarnate life, death, and resurrection that bring salvation to us. Jesus himself said, "Come to me, all you who are weary and burdened, and I will give you rest" (Matt. 11:28).

The cities of refuge were open to all people, Gentiles as well as Jews (Josh. 20:9). In the same way, Jesus Christ saves all kinds of people—Jews and Gentiles, men and women, rich and poor. No one who flees to this city of refuge will be excluded. Jesus said, "All that the Father gives me will come to me, and whoever comes to me I will never drive away" (John 6:37).

Outside the City

What about those who refuse to come to Christ, who remain outside the refuge he offers? The Bible says that outside of Christ are darkness, misery, hopelessness, and eternal death. Jesus said on numerous occasions that unbelievers will be thrown outside, into the darkness, where there will be weeping and gnashing of teeth (Matt. 8:12; 13:42, 50; 25:30).

Although people today mock any preacher who speaks of eternal judgment, the Scriptures clearly teach that there is a heaven and a hell. Heaven is a place of eternal happiness, blessing, and communion with God; it is a place of inexpressible joy and felicity. But hell is a place of eternal and inexpressible misery, pain, and unhappiness.

Revelation 22:15 says, "Outside are the dogs, those who practice magic arts, the sexually immoral, the murderers, the idolaters and everyone who loves and practices falsehood." Outside! There is an outside and there is an inside. Outside is the City of Destruction, but inside is the City of God, the City of Life, the City of Eternal Refuge in Jesus Christ.

Have You Found Refuge?

What about you? Have you fled to the city of refuge? Have you trusted in Jesus Christ? There is a death penalty far more severe than dying at the hands of the avenger of blood. It is the eternal death that awaits every person who is outside of Christ. But there is a way of escape. Jesus says, "I give them eternal life, and they shall never perish" (John 10:28).

Run to him, and run in earnest! There is only one sure escape from the eternal death penalty—only one way, only one Savior, only one city of refuge for all sinners. "Salvation is found in no one else, for there is no other name under heaven given to men by which we must be saved" (Acts 4:12).

No one is going to carry you to Christ; fleeing to him is each person's responsibility. I urge you to wake out of your slumber and see the realities of heaven and hell, sin and judgment, life and death. May the Holy Spirit convict you of your sin, your guilt, your impending judgment, and the punishment due you.

Run now! Do not procrastinate. Now is the accepted time, today is the day of salvation. The city of refuge is open; Jesus Christ still bids you to come. But this will not always be so. In the days of Noah, God warned of a coming flood that would destroy all sinners. He provided an ark of safety for those who desired to escape. We are told that only eight people entered the ark (Gen. 7:13). Then the Lord himself shut the door, and those outside perished.

So too, God has warned in the Scriptures that he will send his Son with glory and power to judge the world. When he comes, he will sit on a throne and summon all men that he may judge them. For most, that judgment will result in condemnation. Only those who have repented of their sins and fled to Jesus Christ will be saved. John 3:36 declares, "Whoever believes in the Son has eternal life, but whoever rejects the Son will not see life, for God's wrath remains on him." Therefore, I urge you to flee to Christ and entrust yourself to him today.

13

The Joy of
Christian Stewardship

Joshua 21

*Now the family heads of the Levites approached Eleazar
the priest, Joshua son of Nun, and the heads of the other
tribal families of Israel at Shiloh in Canaan and said to
them, "The LORD commanded through Moses that you give
us towns to live in, with pasturelands for our livestock."*

*So, as the LORD had commanded, the Israelites gave the
Levites the following towns and pasturelands out of their
own inheritance.*

Joshua 21:1–3

There is a saying, "Lord, keep our pastor
humble, and we will help by keeping him poor." This
attitude should never be found in God's church! Pastors
and teachers are to be supported by God's people from the
abundant provision God has given to them. This method
of financing was true in both Old and New Testament
times, and it is still true today.

In the Old Testament, God appointed the Levites to serve
as his ministers to the nation of Israel. Their sole duties

surrounded the work of the Tent of Meeting. The Levites were to be supported by their fellow citizens through the various means outlined in the Mosaic legislation, including the provision of land. The twenty-first chapter of Joshua recounts the allocation of towns and pasturelands for the Levites in Canaan in keeping with the Lord's instructions to Moses. From this chapter we learn about the responsibilities and joys of Christian stewardship.

The Old Testament Provision for Levites

The principle of Christian giving is exemplified in the Lord's provision for the Levites. The patriarch Levi had three sons: Gershon, Kohath, and Merari. The descendants of these three sons had been set apart by the Lord to assist Aaron and the other priests in performing the work of the tabernacle. The Gershonites were in charge of transporting the coverings and curtains for the tabernacle, the Kohathites were responsible for the furnishings, and the Merarites were responsible for the hardware, especially the frames. The priests, the descendants of Aaron, had the most important responsibilities of all: carrying the ark of the covenant and offering sacrifices. The priests led worship and were assisted by their fellow Levites.

The Levites were not given an allotment of land in Canaan like the other tribes. Rather, the Lord was to be their portion and inheritance, and he would provide for their every need. Numbers 18 and 35 detail the Lord's provision for his ministers:

1. The priests who served at the altar were to receive those portions of the offerings that were not burned up in sacrifice (18:8–20).
2. The Levites were to receive from all the Israelites a tithe (a tenth) of the annual increase from their labor (18:21–24).

3. The Levites, in turn, were to give a tithe of their income to the priests, the descendants of Aaron (18:25–32).

4. The priests and Levites were to receive forty-eight cities, with their pasturelands, as gifts from their fellow Israelites (35:1–5).

Now that Joshua had conquered Canaan and apportioned the land to the tribes, the Levites came forward to claim their cities: "Now the family heads of the Levites approached Eleazar the priest, Joshua son of Nun, and the heads of the other tribal families of Israel at Shiloh in Canaan and said to them, 'The LORD commanded through Moses that you give us towns to live in, with pasturelands for our livestock'" (Josh. 21:1–2). And we are told that the tribes responded in obedience: "So the Israelites allotted to the Levites these towns and their pasturelands as the LORD had commanded through Moses" (v. 8). Tribes with a larger number of cities gave more, so Judah gave nine cities, including Hebron, which Caleb generously donated after conquering it for himself. The other tribes generally gave four cities each, in accordance with the biblical principle of proportional giving.

God finances the work of the kingdom as his people give out of the abundant provisions they have received from him. God's ministers were provided with cities to live in and enough land for their cattle; their ongoing needs were financed by the tithes and offerings of the Israelites. In obedience to divine command, the people gave freely from what God had freely given them.

God does not expect us to give out of nothing! He first blesses us, then directs us how to finance his work and support his workers. David spoke of this principle: "But who am I, and who are my people, that we should be able to give as generously as this? Everything comes from you, and we have given you only what comes from your hand"

(1 Chron. 29:14). When we give, we are only giving back to God a portion of what he has given to us.

When we love God, we will obey his word delightfully and finance the work of his kingdom gladly. We find an illustration of this principle in 2 Chronicles 31. During the reign of Ahaz, the people were in a state of apostasy and the ministers suffered. After Hezekiah came to the throne, however, God brought revival and the king began to enforce biblical law:

> [Hezekiah] ordered the people living in Jerusalem to give the portion due the priests and Levites so they could devote themselves to the Law of the LORD. As soon as the order went out, the Israelites generously gave the firstfruits of their grain, new wine, oil and honey and all that the fields produced. They brought a great amount, a tithe of everything. The men of Israel and Judah who lived in the towns of Judah also brought a tithe of their herds and flocks and a tithe of the holy things dedicated to the LORD their God, and they piled them in heaps. They began doing this in the third month and finished in the seventh month. When Hezekiah and his officials came and saw the heaps, they praised the LORD and blessed his people Israel. Hezekiah asked the priests and Levites about the heaps; and Azariah the chief priest, from the family of Zadok, answered, "Since the people began to bring their contributions to the temple of the LORD, we have had enough to eat and plenty to spare, because the LORD has blessed his people, and this great amount is left over." (2 Chron. 31: 4–11)

God provides abundantly for the work of his kingdom in every age.

Stealing God's Tithe

The emphasis God places on giving and tithing highlights the importance of practicing Christian stewardship. Though all things belong to him, the tithe

128

does so especially. "A tithe of everything from the land, whether grain from the soil or fruit from the trees, belongs to the LORD; it is holy to the LORD" (Lev. 27:30). "Holy to the Lord" means something belongs exclusively to God. The story of Achan in Joshua 7 stands forever as a warning against taking that which belongs to God.

Later, in post-exilic times, God chastised the whole nation of Israel for robbing him with respect to the tithes and offerings:

> "Will a man rob God? Yet you rob me. But you ask, 'How do we rob you?' In tithes and offerings. You are under a curse—the whole nation of you—because you are robbing me. Bring the whole tithe into the storehouse, that there may be food in my house. Test me in this," says the Lord Almighty, "and see if I will not throw open the floodgates of heaven and pour out so much blessing that you will not have room enough for it. I will prevent pests from devouring your crops, and the vines in your fields will not cast their fruit." (Mal. 3:8–11)

God had sent drought and pests and had withheld his blessing from his people because they were stealing from him. He promised to restore those blessings once his people responded in obedience.

What happens today if God's people refuse to give God what belongs to him? Does he have a collection agency? Indeed, he does. God still relates to his people on the basis of the covenant he made with them. When we keep his covenant, we are blessed; but when we refuse to obey, we are cursed. "'Cursed is the cheat who has an acceptable male in his flock and vows to give it, but then sacrifices a blemished animal to the Lord. For I am a great king,' says the LORD Almighty, 'and my name is to be feared among the nations'" (Mal. 1:14). The curse threatened in the covenant comes to those who rob God and treat him with disrespect.

The post-exilic prophecy of Haggai describes how God disciplined those of his covenant people who dishonored him by withholding their tithe:

> "You have planted much, but have harvested little. You eat, but never have enough. You drink, but never have your fill. You put on clothes, but are not warm. You earn wages, only to put them in a purse with holes in it. . . . You expected much, but see, it turned out to be little. What you brought home, I blew away. Why?" declares the Lord Almighty. "Because of my house, which remains a ruin, while each of you is busy with his own house. Therefore, because of you the heavens have withheld their dew and the earth its crops. I called for a drought on the fields and the mountains, on the grain, the new wine, the oil and whatever the ground produces, on men and cattle, and on the labor of your hands." (Hag. 1:6, 9–11)

God knows how and where to apply pressure until we fulfill our responsibility as stewards.

Just as God's threatenings are sure, so also are his covenant promises. If we obey the Lord's command to tithe, he will bless us. As we have read in Malachi 3:10, God promises he will "pour out so much blessing that you will not have room enough for it."

The New Testament Provision for Leaders

Despite what many modern churchgoers may think about tithing, the New Testament clearly states that those who preach the gospel deserve to be supported. Consider the words of Jesus Christ to his disciples: "Do not take along any gold or silver or copper in your belts; take no bag for the journey, or extra tunic, or sandals or a staff; for the worker is worth his keep" (Matt. 10:9–10). Notice, it says the *worker* is worth his keep. A minister who toils and labors for the flock is worthy of remuneration. Jesus elsewhere said, "The worker deserves his wages" (Luke 10:7). Supporting one's minister is not a matter of charity or feeling sorry for him. No! The hardworking minister deserves his pay.

The apostle Paul further elaborates on this key concept:

> This is my defense to those who sit in judgment on me. Don't we have the right to food and drink? Don't we have the right to take a believing wife along with us, as do the other apostles and the Lord's brothers and Cephas? Or is it only I and Barnabas who must work for a living?
>
> Who serves as a soldier at his own expense? Who plants a vineyard and does not eat of its grapes? Who tends a flock and does not drink of the milk? Do I say this merely from a human point of view? Doesn't the Law say the same thing? For it is written in the Law of Moses: "Do not muzzle an ox while it is treading out the grain." Is it about oxen that God is concerned? Surely he says this for us, doesn't he? Yes, this was written for us, because when the plowman plows and the thresher threshes, they ought to do so in the hope of sharing in the harvest. If we have sown spiritual seed among you, is it too much if we reap a material harvest from you? If others have this right of support from you, shouldn't we have it all the more?
>
> But we did not use this right. On the contrary, we put up with anything rather than hinder the gospel of Christ. Don't you know that those who work in the temple get their food from the temple, and those who serve at the altar share in what is offered on the altar? In the same way, the Lord has commanded that those who preach the gospel should receive their living from the gospel. (1 Cor. 9:3–14)

In this passage the Greek word for "right" is used multiple times. A minister has a God-given right to be supported by his congregation. Just as a soldier is supported entirely by his government, and a farmer lives off the fruit of his labors, so too should the minister who labors as a shepherd on behalf of the Good Shepherd be provided for by his flock.

Not only do church leaders deserve financial support from their congregation, but they also are entitled to their respect. Paul wrote to the church at Thessalonica, "Now we ask you, brothers, to respect those who work hard among you, who are over you in the Lord and who admonish you. Hold them in the highest regard in love because of their work" (1 Thess. 5:12–13). The Greek word for "highest" is used only two other times in the New Testament—once in Ephesians 3:20, where Paul says God is "able to do *exceedingly abundantly* above all that we ask or think" (KJV), and once in 1 Thessalonians 3:10, where Paul says, "Night and day we pray *most earnestly*" (italics added). There is no more powerful adverb in all of Scripture. We are not to worship God's ministers, for we worship God alone, but we must hold them in the highest esteem.

Paul later wrote to Timothy, a fellow minister of the gospel, to help him in the task of bringing order to the early churches: "The elders who direct the affairs of the church well are worthy of double honor, especially those whose work is preaching and teaching. For the Scripture says, 'Do not muzzle the ox while it is treading out the grain,' and 'The worker deserves his wages'" (1 Tim. 5:17–18). What does "double honor" mean? John Stott argues correctly that it means respect and remuneration (*Guard the Truth*, 77). Both are necessary. If we do not respect someone, then we will not respond to that person's proclamation. Respect is essential for learning from a teacher, pastor, father, or mother. And remuneration is part of respect. After all, a pastor cannot eat respect!

Principles of Christian Stewardship

In light of what we have learned, what are some principles of Christian stewardship?

First, we must understand that the Lord's financing program consists of our tithes and offerings. How much are we supposed to give? The tithe is a fixed amount, one-tenth of our income, and the offering can be any amount we decide. Note that even God's ministers are expected to tithe, as the Lord commanded the Levites: "When you receive from the Israelites the tithe I give you as your inheritance, you must present a tenth of that tithe as the LORD's offering" (Num. 18:26).

Second, we must give regularly. To give only when we feel like it is not right. The Levites received daily food. Just so, a minister has to live; he cannot depend solely on people's generous feelings. Paul instructed the New Testament believers, "On the first day of every week, each one of you should set aside a sum of money in keeping with his income" (1 Cor. 16:2).

Third, giving should be in proportion to our income. Just as the tribes with more land gave the Levites more cities, so we are to give in accordance with the measure God has prospered us. "No man should appear before the LORD empty-handed: Each of you must bring a gift in proportion to the way the LORD your God has blessed you" (Deut. 16:16–17).

If you have never experienced the joy of giving, I encourage you to start today. "Give, and it will be given to you. A good measure, pressed down, shaken together and running over, will be poured into your lap. For with the measure you use, it will be measured to you" (Luke 6:38). Not only does God bless your giving here on earth, but you are also storing up treasure in heaven.

Keep in mind the generosity of Christ. "For you know the grace of our Lord Jesus Christ, that though he was rich, yet for your sakes he became poor, so that you through his poverty might become rich" (2 Cor. 8:9). Paul exclaims, "Thanks be to God for his indescribable gift!" (2 Cor. 9:15). Elsewhere we read, "He who did not spare his own Son, but gave him up for us all—how will he not also, along with him, graciously give us all things?" (Rom. 8:32). Have you received God's greatest gift of his Son, Jesus Christ? Receive him as your Lord and Savior. He will provide for you generously and will make you a generous giver. Through him you will gladly give, even your own life, for the sake of the gospel.

14

The Faithfulness of the Covenant Lord

Joshua 23

Be very strong; be careful to obey all that is written in the Book of the Law of Moses, without turning aside to the right or to the left. . . . You are to hold fast to the LORD your God, as you have until now.

Joshua 23:6, 8

The last two chapters of the book of Joshua record the farewell address of Joshua, the faithful servant of the Lord. We should always listen closely to the last words of a mature, God-fearing person, for they convey what is most essential for life. Joshua's final message to the Israelites was that they should continue to look to the covenant Lord, the God who had been faithful in the past, was faithful in the present, and would be faithful in the future.

Joshua was now nearly 110 years of age, and he knew he was about to die. He himself stated, "Now I am about to go the way of all the earth" (Josh. 23:14). He had earned the right to give his final words of wisdom to the assembly, for he had lived an obedient, holy life. As a young man, he had been an eyewitness to God's miraculous works. He had seen the ten plagues in Egypt and the parting of the Red Sea. He had seen the pillar of cloud and the pillar of fire guiding Israel. He had drunk the water from the flinty rock and had eaten manna for forty years. He had also seen his fellow Israelites die in the desert as God executed judgment on them. Throughout all this, Joshua had obeyed the Lord fully, never murmuring against him. When the other spies discouraged the people, Joshua had given a good report. He had fought valiantly against the Amalekites and Amorites in the desert, and had conquered Canaan after crossing the Jordan. Joshua had a different spirit—the Holy Spirit— and was commended by the Lord as a good and faithful servant. It is indeed wise to heed the final counsel of such a faithful servant of the Lord.

"Look to the Lord!"

Verse 2 says that Joshua summoned all the leaders of Israel to encourage them even as he himself had earlier been exhorted by the Lord after the death of Moses. At that time the Lord had said to Joshua:

> Be strong and courageous, because you will lead these people to inherit the land I swore to their forefathers to give them. Be strong and very courageous. Be careful to obey all the law my servant Moses gave you; do not turn from it to the right or to the left, that you may be successful wherever you go. Do not let this Book of the Law depart from your mouth; meditate on it day and night, so that you may be careful to do everything written in it. Then you will be prosperous and successful. Have I not commanded you? Be strong and courageous. Do not be terrified; do not be discouraged, for the Lord your God will be with you wherever you go. (Josh. 1:6–9)

What counsel did Joshua give? He pointed the people to God. In the sixteen verses of Joshua 23, Joshua cited the name of Yahweh (or LORD) seventeen times. He, in effect, was saying, "Don't look to me, for I am old and dying. And do not look to anyone else. Look to the Lord of the covenant and follow him, for he alone is the undying, everlasting one." Joshua focused the people's attention on Yahweh, the self-existing God, who is unchanging in his being and in his relationship with his people. This is the counsel God himself gives us in Isaiah 45:22: "Look unto me, and be ye saved, all the ends of the earth: for I am God, and there is none else" (KJV).

Yahweh is the gracious God, the covenant Lord and Savior who saves his people by his mighty deeds. He is the Sovereign Lord who controls all history and the universe. This Yahweh demands total loyalty of his people. To disobey him is disastrous, but to obey him is to enjoy great salvation. Joshua reminded the people of Yahweh's dealings with them in the past, called attention to Yahweh's faithfulness in the present, and assured them of Yahweh's faithfulness in the future. Although Joshua must die, the Lord who lives forever would lead his people, not only into rest in Canaan, but also into the eternal rest of heaven.

Faithful in the Past

In order to appreciate God's faithfulness, we must first review our salvation history, as the elderly Joshua now did with the people of Israel: "You yourselves have seen everything the LORD your God has done" (v. 3). Years earlier, the Lord of the covenant had appeared to Moses in the burning bush and commissioned him to deliver Israel from her Egyptian slavery. The Lord had brought his people out of Egypt by his mighty deeds, leading them, feeding them, protecting them, and finally bringing them into the promised land of Canaan. There the Lord had fought for them, conquering the land and giving it to them as an inheritance.

Clearly, God had been faithful to his people in the past, giving them the land of Canaan with its cities to live in (vv. 13, 15–16). Israel was to reflect on the Lord's faithfulness in the past so that they would now trust him in the present. Joshua emphasized several points in this regard:

1. *God gave them rest.* "The LORD gave them rest on every side, just as he had sworn to their forefathers. Not one of their enemies withstood them" (Josh. 21:44). Joshua told the people, "You yourselves have seen everything the LORD your God has done to all these nations for your sake" (23:3). They were eyewitnesses to the Lord's miraculous saving deeds that had brought them into the land of promise.

2. *God fought for them.* Joshua reminded the people in verse 3, "It was the LORD your God who fought for you." In other words, they did not give themselves this rest; it was a result of God fighting for them. And he who fought for them in the past would fight for them in the present and in the future.

3. *The Lord drove out their enemies.* Joshua told the people, "The LORD has driven out before you great and powerful nations; to this day no one has been able to withstand you" (23:9). He wanted to assure the people that their God was greater than the Egyptians, Amalekites, Amorites, and all other nations and their idols.

4. *The Lord was faithful to all his promises.* "Not one of all the LORD's good promises to the house of Israel failed; every one was fulfilled" (Josh. 21:45). Unlike human beings, God does not forget what he has promised. He does not lie or change his mind (Num. 23:19; 1 Sam. 15:29). What God promises, he fulfills. Therefore Joshua declared, "Now I am about to go the way of all the earth. You know with all

your heart and soul that not one of all the good promises the LORD your God gave you has failed. Every promise has been fulfilled; not one has failed" (Josh. 23:14).

This, then, was the first part of Joshua's farewell counsel: Look back and see the faithfulness of God, and know that God always does what he has promised. He has done so in the past, he is doing so now, and he will do so in the future.

Faithful in the Present

We cannot change the past, nor can we control the future, but we can focus our attention on the present. We must do the will of God today, knowing that he is with us. Continuing his speech, Joshua now focused on the present imperatives for the people of God in light of God's faithfulness:

1. *We must obey the Scriptures.* "Be careful to obey all that is written in the Book of the Law of Moses, without turning aside to the right or to the left" (v. 6). We are the people of the Scriptures, and each day we must read them, study them, meditate upon them, and do what they say. We must not think that God will fight for us whether we obey him or not. As the Sovereign Lord, our God demands complete loyalty and obedience from his people.

2. *We must be separate.* Joshua told the people, "Do not associate with these nations that remain among you; do not invoke the names of their gods or swear by them. You must not serve them or bow down to them" (23:7), for that is idolatry. God commands his people in every generation to separate themselves from the pagan world.

God left some of the nations within Canaan to test the Israelites, to see whether his people would demonstrate their love for him by serving him and worshiping him only. Joshua warned the congregation: "But if you turn away and ally yourselves with the survivors of these nations that remain among you and if you intermarry with them and associate with them, then you may be sure that the LORD your God will no longer drive out these nations before you" (vv. 12–13).

In 2 Corinthians 6:14–18 the apostle Paul exhorts, "Do not be yoked together with unbelievers." This applies to unbelievers in the church as well as unbelievers in the world. Then he asks, "For what do righteousness and wickedness have in common?" What is the expected answer? Nothing! "Or what fellowship can light have with darkness?" None! "What harmony is there between Christ and Belial?" None! "What does a believer have in common with an unbeliever?" Nothing, except for our responsibility to declare the gospel to them. "What agreement is there between the temple of God and idols?" None! "For we are the temple of the living God. As God has said: 'I will live with them and walk among them, and I will be their God, and they will be my people.' 'Therefore come out from them and be separate,' says the Lord. 'Touch no unclean thing, and I will receive you.' 'I will be a Father to you, and you will be my sons and daughters,' says the Lord Almighty." God's people are to be separate, living in the world but not living like the world.

3. *We must love, obey, and hold fast to God.* Joshua told the people, "But you are to hold fast to the LORD" (v. 8). The word for "hold fast" is also used in Genesis 2:24 with reference to marriage: one must leave one's father and mother and cleave to, or be joined to, or hold fast to, one's spouse. It is the language of intimacy and communion, the language of exclusive love. As Jesus said in John 15, we must abide in Christ, as a branch abides in the vine. This is vital union with Christ. He is our husband and we are his wife, and there must be no adultery or idolatry. Our covenant Lord delivered us from Egypt, and we must have no other gods before him.

Joshua further told the people, "Be very careful to love the LORD your God" (v. 11). Joshua earlier had given a clear definition of what it means to love God and hold fast to him when he spoke to the eastern tribes: "Be very careful to keep the commandment and the law that Moses the servant of the LORD gave you: to love the LORD your God, to walk in all his ways, to obey his commands, to hold fast to him and to serve him with all your heart and all your soul" (Josh. 22:5). In other words, love for God is keeping God's commandments. Jesus Christ said, "If you love me, you will obey what I command" (John 14:15).

We love God because he first loved us. As Moses told the Israelites, "The LORD did not set his affection on you and choose you because you were more numerous than other peoples, for you were the fewest of all peoples. But it was because the LORD loved you and kept the oath he swore to your forefathers that he brought you out with a mighty hand and redeemed you from the land of slavery" (Deut. 7:7–8). Because God first loved us, he saved us, redeemed us, fought for us, and gave us rest. No other god or man did these things. Since the Sovereign Lord alone did these things for us, we must love him in return.

4. *We must look to the Lord to fight our battles.* In our battle against sin and Satan, we have to keep in mind that we are not fighting by ourselves. Yes, we are to fight, but we do so in conjunction with the Lord. We are strengthened and energized to win, but we must never credit ourselves. We are victorious because the Lord fights for us.

Note how verse 3 speaks of the past: "It was the LORD your God who fought for you," while verse 10 speaks of the present: "One of you routs a thousand, because the LORD your God fights for you, just as he promised." God fought and God fights! As we think about God's faithfulness to his covenant in the past, we will be strengthened and encouraged in the present. We need not fear our enemies, for we know the Sovereign Lord is for us.

Faithful in the Future

Finally, Joshua spoke about the future: "The LORD your God himself will drive them out of your way. He will push them out before you, and you will take possession of their land, as the LORD your God promised you" (v. 5). We tend to be fearful and anxious about what will happen to us. But if we live for God in the present, we need not worry about tomorrow. The Lord who fought for us in the past and who fights for us in the present will surely fight for us in the future. We have been saved, we are being saved, and we will be saved.

In Joshua 1:5 the Lord told Joshua, "No one will be able to stand up against you all the days of your life. As I was with Moses, so I will be with you; I will never leave you nor forsake you." Likewise, the Lord Jesus Christ tells those who are his, "Surely I am with you always, to the very end of the age" (Matt. 28:20). Our God is not just the God of the past or the present, but he is also the God of the future. He will be with us even at the moment of our death, giving us strength to die in hope.

Those who are obedient to God have nothing to fear, for they will experience covenant blessings from their covenant Lord. But those who are disobedient should fear, for they will experience divine curse and divine judgment unless they repent. Joshua solemnly warned the gathered Israelites, "If you violate the covenant of the LORD your God, which he commanded you, and go and serve other gods and bow down to them, the LORD's anger will burn against you, and you will quickly perish from the good land he has given you" (v. 16). God's anger will burn against his own people, not pagans, if they do not obey him. The Israelites did in fact come under the cruel domination of their neighbors and eventually ceased to be a nation for precisely this reason.

Jesus Christ, the Greater Joshua

In God's plan, Joshua brought Israel to the rest of Canaan. He could not, however, grant them the rest of forgiveness, justification, and peace with a holy God. Joshua son of Nun could not make atonement for the sins of Israel, because he himself was a sinner in need of salvation. To receive the rest of forgiveness and restoration of communion with God, we must look to another Joshua—one who is greater than Joshua son of Nun, one who is greater than Moses, one who is greater than all men. We must look to Jesus Christ, the son of Abraham, the son of David, the son of Mary, the son of God.

Jesus Christ is the Lamb of God who has taken away our sins by his death on our behalf. He calls to all sinners, saying, "Come to me, all you who are weary and burdened, and I will give you rest. Take my yoke upon you and learn from me, for I am gentle and humble in heart, and you will find rest for your souls. For my yoke is easy and my burden is light" (Matt. 11:28–30). Jesus Christ, the undying eternal One, died as an atoning sacrifice for our sins. He alone gives rest to our souls the moment we trust in him, and he continues to give us rest as we walk in daily obedience to him. When our work on earth is done, our Good Shepherd will bring us to eternal rest with him.

The people of Israel enjoyed a certain rest when they received their portion of land in Canaan, but the rest Christ gives us has nothing to do with real estate. Paul spoke of this greater rest: "I desire to depart and be with Christ, which is better by far" (Phil. 1:23). So the farewell message of Joshua son of Nun to us is this: "Look not to me, but to the greater Joshua, Jesus Christ. He is the Lord of salvation, and he will give you the true rest of heaven." The future rest for believers is eternal glory and everlasting bliss. It is living in the house of the Lord and seeing him face to face. It is joy unspeakable and full of glory. It is life with Christ forever.

I encourage you to reflect upon your own past and see how God has been gracious to you. I exhort you to look at the Scripture and see what the Lord has done for you. Christ has triumphed over all our enemies by his death on the cross, and now he gives us rest. The risen and reigning Christ is with us now, fighting all our battles. Look to him daily by faith! Not only is Christ with us now, but he also will be with us in the future, and he will lead us into his everlasting rest.

15

I and My Family Will Serve the Lord

Joshua 24

Now fear the LORD and serve him with all faithfulness. Throw away the gods your forefathers worshiped beyond the River and in Egypt, and serve the LORD. But if serving the LORD seems undesirable to you, then choose for yourselves this day whom you will serve, whether the gods your forefathers served beyond the River, or the gods of the Amorites, in whose land you are living. But as for me and my household, we will serve the LORD.

Joshua 24:14–15

Having reminded the people of God's covenant faithfulness, Joshua summoned all Israel to a final meeting at Shechem to renew their covenant with the Lord. He called upon them to make the most important decision any of us will ever make: "Choose for yourselves this day whom you will serve." Joshua himself resolutely declared, "As for me and my household, we will serve the Lord."

The final chapter in the book of Joshua is a lesson about covenant-keeping families. Modern culture destroys families. The courts, the government, the educational system, and even some churches undermine family structure, authority, and values. But God is for families; he is interested in saving not only individuals, but also entire households: "The promise is for you and your children" (Acts 2:39).

Why is it important to be a covenant-keeping family? Because the Lord deals with his people based on covenant. Covenant relationship is basic to Christianity, as we see throughout the Scriptures. There is one Lord, one people of God, one way of salvation, and one covenant between God and his people.

The Covenant of the Lord

God requires his people to renew the covenant they made with him periodically. Deuteronomy 29–30, for example, relates how all Israel assembled together before Moses' death for this very purpose. Joshua 24 begins with the people of Israel again presenting themselves before God for covenant renewal.

Many scholars view this chapter in the light of the covenant structure that prevailed among the Hittites in the second millennium BC. At that time, covenants called *suzerainty treaties* were often established between a great king (the suzerain) and his underlings (the vassals). These were not treaties between equal partners. The great king alone would write the terms of the covenant, and the vassals must fully accept his terms and obey them. Likewise, the people of Israel were obligated to re-affirm their loyalty and obedience to their great king, the Lord God Almighty.

The elements of a suzerainty treaty are as follows:

1. The preamble, wherein the overlord identifies himself by name;

2. The historical prologue, wherein the lord of the covenant reviews his relationship with his vassals, detailing how he helped them in the past;
3. The stipulations, or terms of the covenant, in which the suzerain demands that his vassals remain loyal to him by obeying these terms;
4. The sanctions, which are the blessings for obedience and curses for disobedience.

Joshua 24 is a highly condensed version of the covenant God had previously made with the people of Israel.

The Preamble

Joshua began with the covenantal preamble: "This is what the LORD, the God of Israel, says . . ." (v. 2). Here the Lord, the great king, is identified. We see the same identification in Exodus 20:2: "I am the LORD your God." The Lord of the preamble is the God of Israel, the Lord who appeared to Moses in the burning bush, the "I AM." He is the unchanging, eternal, sovereign God who does not age or weaken.

This true and living God, unlike the false gods of the nations, is moral and holy. He declares himself to be "the LORD, the LORD, the compassionate and gracious God, slow to anger, abounding in love and faithfulness, maintaining love to thousands, and forgiving wickedness, rebellion and sin. Yet he does not leave the guilty unpunished; he punishes the children and their children for the sin of the fathers to the third and fourth generation" (Exod. 34:6–7).

People love idols because they permit them to sin. But the Scriptures tell us that behind these idols stand Satan and his demonic powers: "They sacrificed to demons, which are not God—gods they had not known, gods that recently appeared, gods your fathers did not fear"

(Deut. 32:17). The God of the covenant becomes jealous when his people give their loyalty to demons.

The Historical Prologue

Joshua continued his address by turning to the historical prologue: "Long ago your forefathers, including Terah the father of Abraham and Nahor, lived beyond the River and worshiped other gods. But I took your father Abraham from the land beyond the River and led him throughout Canaan and gave him many descendants" (vv. 2–3) This section (vv. 2–13) reviews Israel's salvation history, telling how the Lord took the initiative to save his wretched people. The Lord speaks in "I/thou" terms here, using the pronoun "I" eighteen times in reference to the various saving deeds he performed in behalf of his people.

The God of glory appeared to Abraham in Mesopotamia, not when he was righteous, but when he was still a worshipper of the moon god Sin. The Lord led Abraham out of Mesopotamia and into Canaan. It was the Lord who took the initiative, seeking and saving Abraham when he was an unrighteous idolater. Moreover, it was the Lord who took the initiative throughout Israel's history. The Lord gave Abraham children, and chose Isaac and later Jacob. The Lord sent Jacob and his children to Egypt, then sent Moses and Aaron centuries later to deliver their descendants. The Lord afflicted the Egyptians with plagues and defeated all the Egyptian gods. The Lord brought Israel out safely through the Red Sea while destroying the Egyptians. The Lord destroyed the Amorite kings of Sihon and Og. The Lord defeated Balak by turning the curses of Balaam into one blessing after another.

As the captain of the Lord's army, the Lord defeated all Israel's enemies. He told the Israelites, "I sent the hornet ahead of you, which drove them out before you. . . . You did not do it with your own sword and bow" (Josh. 24:12).

Finally, the Lord gave his people rest: "So I gave you a land on which you did not toil and cities you did not build; and you live in them and eat from vineyards and olive groves that you did not plant" (v. 13).

The Sovereign Lord had taken care of Israel for over half a millennium. He defeated the gods of the Egyptians, Amalekites, and Amorites. He saved his people and defeated all his enemies. And he continues to do so today. Christ loves the church and gave himself for her salvation. Just as God chose the pagan Abraham and granted him saving faith, so he still chooses sinners to be saved, making those who are dead in their sins alive in Christ. He does so by grace, not because of any merit on the part of the sinner. Salvation is by grace alone through faith alone from beginning to end.

Think about what the Lord has done for us! Think of our election in Christ before the creation of the world. Though we were born sinners, God gave us grace and led us every step of the way, giving us food and clothing, health and well-being. God defeated our enemies, preserving and protecting us. God caused us to hear the gospel and regenerated us, granting us the gift of repentance and saving faith. God prepared a Bible for us to read, that we might discover his will and do it delightfully. This same Lord will guide us to the end of our life and bring us into his presence, without fault, in exceeding glory and joy. How great is the love the Lord has lavished upon us!

The Stipulations

In the suzerainty treaty, the king put certain stipulations upon his vassals. Joshua articulated the following divine covenant stipulations in verses 14–24:

1. FEAR THE LORD
The first stipulation is found in verse 14: "Now fear the LORD." "Now" means in the light of all that God has

done for us by his personal initiative and power. We are dependent upon God's love, mercy, power, and covenant faithfulness; therefore, we must fear him.

The fear of the Lord is the beginning of wisdom (Ps. 111:10), and the fear of the Lord keeps us from sinning (Exod. 20:20). When we sin, we are treating the covenant Lord with contempt. The Bible warns those who would continue in sin that it is a dreadful thing to fall into the hands of the living God, who is a consuming fire (Heb. 10:31; 12:29). The key to a holy life is to have reverence for God, to whom we all must give an account. Such fear should lead us to submit to the Lord's will eagerly, just as a son who reveres his father will be eager to please him by doing his father's will.

Isaiah 11:2–3 foretells about Jesus, "The Spirit of the LORD will rest on him—the Spirit of wisdom and of understanding, the Spirit of counsel and of power, the Spirit of knowledge and of the fear of the LORD—and he will delight in the fear of the LORD." Since Jesus Christ was filled and directed by the Spirit of the fear of the Lord, he always did the Father's will. Jesus himself declared, "Father . . . I have brought you glory on earth by completing the work you gave me to do" (John 17:4). It was his great pleasure to do the will of God, for he said, "My food is to do the will of him who sent me and to finish his work" (John 4:34), and "I always do what pleases him" (John 8:29). Finally, he prayed to his Father, "Not my will, but yours be done" (Luke 22:42), and he gave his life in obedience to the Father's will in order to save us.

2. SERVE THE LORD

The second stipulation is also found in verse 14: "Now fear the LORD and serve him with all faithfulness." We are to serve the Lord exclusively in covenant fidelity. The covenant relationship can be summed up in a single statement: "I am the Lord, and you are my servant." In fact, the Hebrew word meaning "to serve" appears sixteen times in this chapter, eleven times referring to serving the Lord exclusively. The same relationship is found in the New Testament. In Romans 1:1 the apostle Paul introduces himself as a bondservant of Christ. As Christians, we make the same declaration: "Jesus is Lord," meaning that he is the Lord and we are his servants, who serve him exclusively.

Everyone is a servant. Either we serve demons or we serve the true and living God. The heart of Christianity is to serve the covenant Lord who has saved us from our slavery to sin. There is a false theology rampant in churches today that says, "Receive Jesus into your heart as Savior, and then one day you can put him on the throne of your heart." This implies that we can receive Christ and carry on a sinful life until we want to make him Lord. This is not the true gospel! Jesus Christ is the sovereign Lord of the covenant who demands obedience to his stipulations. He is Savior *because* he is Lord.

We are commanded in Joshua 24:14 to serve the Lord "with all faithfulness," meaning in sincerity and truth. We are to serve him, not based on our changing feelings, but on the basis of the objective, written covenant document—the word of God. If we are true believers, we will embrace God's word and say, "The Lord commands it; therefore, I will obey it with pleasure, because of what my covenant Lord has done for me."

Three times the people responded, "We will serve the Lord" (24:18, 21, 24), meaning, "We will serve the Lord exclusively in covenant fidelity." This must be our daily response to God and his word as well. Ephesians 2:10 says, "For we are God's workmanship, created in Christ Jesus to do good works, which God prepared in advance for us to do." If we are born of God, we will delight in serving and pleasing him.

3. THROW AWAY IDOLS

The third stipulation states, "Throw away the gods your forefathers worshiped beyond the River and in Egypt, and serve the LORD" (v. 14). In the Hittite treaties, the vassal was to forsake all other alliances and promise that he would serve the great king exclusively. So Joshua told the people a second time, in verse 23, "Throw away the foreign gods that are among you."

This tendency to cling to idols was not unique to Joshua's day. Genesis 35:1 records the Lord's command to Jacob: "Go up to Bethel and settle there, and build an altar there to God." God wanted Jacob and his family to go up to Bethel, the house of God, so they could have fellowship with him there. However, Jacob knew that his family still had idols and therefore could not have fellowship with God. In fact, his own wife Rachel had stolen her father's household gods and hidden them (Gen. 31:19). "So Jacob said to his household and to all who were with him, 'Get rid of the foreign gods you have with you, and purify yourselves and change your clothes'" (Gen. 35:2). The people responded by giving Jacob all the foreign idols they had, and Jacob buried them.

Why would God's people cling to idols? First, for insurance—the people reasoned that if the Lord failed, at least they would have their idols. Second, for pleasure—idols provide enjoyment, if only the deceptive thrill of sin for a season. But it is an utter impossibility to serve both the Lord and idols. God demands exclusive covenant love and obedience. We must examine our own hearts to discover what idols we are serving today. Do not think that you have none! Simply put, an idol is anything or anyone we love more than we love God. The chief idol that competes for our loyalty is self; we tend to prefer our will over God's. Or we may worship our children, our careers, our hobbies, and our money. Nothing in all of creation, however, should be nearer and dearer to us than the Lord of creation.

The Sanctions

In a suzerainty treaty the sanctions are always the same: blessings for obedience and curses for disobedience. Therefore, Joshua warned the people, "You are not able to serve the LORD. He is a holy God; he is a jealous God. He will not forgive your rebellion and your sins. If you forsake the LORD and serve foreign gods, he will turn and bring disaster on you and make an end of you, after he has been good to you" (vv. 19–20).

Moses had described the covenant sanctions in greater detail in Deuteronomy 28–30. "The LORD will send on you curses, confusion and rebuke in everything you put your hand to, until you are destroyed and come to sudden ruin because of the evil you have done in forsaking him. The LORD will plague you with diseases until he has destroyed you from the land you are entering to possess. The LORD will strike you with wasting disease, with fever and inflammation, with scorching heat and drought, with blight and mildew, which will plague you until you perish" (Deut. 28:20–22).

After speaking of these sanctions, Moses told the people, "Take to heart all the words I have solemnly declared to you this day, so that you may command your children to obey carefully all the words of this law. They are not just idle words for you—they are your life. By them you will live long in the land you are crossing the Jordan to possess" (Deut. 32:46–47).

The people of Joshua's era did keep the Lord's covenant: "Israel served the LORD throughout the lifetime of Joshua and of the elders who outlived him and who had experienced everything the LORD had done for Israel" (Josh. 24:31). But Judges 2 tells us what happened to their children:

> After that whole generation had been gathered to their fathers, another generation grew up, who knew neither the LORD nor what he had done for Israel. Then the

Israelites did evil in the eyes of the LORD and served the Baals. They forsook the LORD, the God of their fathers, who had brought them out of Egypt. They followed and worshiped various gods of the people around them. They provoked the LORD to anger because they forsook him and served Baal and the Ashtoreths. In his anger against Israel the LORD handed them over to raiders who plundered them. He sold them to their enemies all around, whom they were no longer able to resist. (Judg. 2:10–14)

The Lord first sold them to the neighboring peoples; then the whole northern kingdom went into exile in 721 BC. The southern kingdom went to Babylon as slaves in 587 BC. Finally, in AD 70, Jerusalem was destroyed by the Romans. God's sanctions are sure and true.

Choose Whom You Will Serve

Joshua said to the people, "But if serving the LORD seems undesirable to you, then choose for yourselves this day whom you will serve, whether the gods your forefathers served beyond the River, or the gods of the Amorites, in whose land you are living. But as for me and my household, we will serve the LORD" (v. 15).

We must decide this very day whom we will serve. Not to choose is to decide in favor of idols, in favor of false gods, in favor of the devil and his demons, in favor of a lifestyle of sin that leads to self-destruction. We can be certain of this: our choice will have consequences. People often lament that they have to live with the consequences of the bad decisions they made in their youth. The decisions we make affect us for the rest of our lives. We must choose wisely, because our choices issue either in blessing or curse.

Joshua exhorts, "Choose for yourselves this day." What is the choice? We must choose between eternal life and eternal damnation. We must choose between serving idols and serving the true and living God. We must decide either to serve the Lord or the devil. This should not be a difficult decision; after all, what have false gods ever done for us? The devil's historical prologue is one disaster after another. As Jesus said, "The thief comes only to steal and kill and destroy" (John 10:10). Sin does nothing to build us up. It can only destroy us physically, economically, and spiritually.

Joshua's own choice is recorded in the last line of verse 15: "But as for me . . ." In the Hebrew it is emphasized: "I myself." Joshua was not attempting to coerce these people. He was saying, in effect, "You can do whatever you want. . . . But as for me and my family, we will serve the Lord." Joshua's resolution was firm. He had chosen the Lord once-for-all while he was in Egypt, after hearing the good news proclaimed by Moses and Aaron that God was going to redeem his people. Likewise, every Christian makes a once-for-all choice the moment he savingly trusts in Jesus Christ.

Additionally, Joshua chose God daily, moment by moment. That must also be true of us. We must choose on a daily basis to do the will of God over against the will of the devil. There is no third way. It should not be difficult to choose between the devil and the Sovereign Lord, Creator, Redeemer, and Eternal Judge of all the earth!

Covenant and Family

Joshua next spoke about his family. Although the names of his wife and children are not mentioned in the Bible, we can conclude that they were godly. Joshua's wife was not like Job's wife, who told her husband, "Curse God and die!" (Job 2:9). Nor was she like Lot's wife, who refused to believe the gospel proclaimed by the angel and was turned to salt (Gen. 19:26). How tragic it is when spiritually-minded people are married to spouses who do not want to serve God. Such families are full of confusion. But Joshua's wife was a godly woman who loved the Lord and raised children who feared the Lord.

Joshua solemnly declared that his household would serve the Lord. Thus, we can conclude that Joshua's children also confessed the name of the Lord. They were covenant-keepers who feared God and ordered their lives in accordance with their father's godly example and biblical teaching. Though Joshua had great national responsibilities as a general and a judge, he did not neglect his family. He was a prophet, priest, and king at home. He was able to govern the whole nation because he governed his own home well.

Paul speaks of the qualifications for a good leader: "He must manage his own family well and see that his children obey him with proper respect. (If anyone does not know how to manage his own family, how can he take care of God's church?)" (1 Tim. 3:4–5). We are living at a time when fewer and fewer men govern their own families. So I ask you, fathers—at a time when many churches have become idolatrous and when people worship the idols of pleasure and possessions, can you say, "I choose to serve the Lord now and forever"? Can you say, "I and my wife and my children all together choose to serve the Lord now and forever"?

God is interested not only in individuals, but also in their families. God saved Joshua and his family. At Philippi the Lord saved Lydia and the members of her household (Acts 16:15). The Lord saved the Philippian jailer and his entire family (Acts 16:31–34). What about your family? Do your children serve the Lord exclusively, or do they serve God and Baal? Awake, O father! Awake, O mother! Choose today to serve the Lord, and him only. Resolve today to say with Joshua, "As for me and my family, we will serve the Lord."

A Final Exhortation

I plead with you to listen to the final words of Joshua. They are not empty words; they are the very words of God that, if heeded, will give us life. The Lord of the covenant has demonstrated his love for us by sending his Son to die on the cross. He is our Savior and our Lord. Let us reflect on our lives and marvel at the great mercy and love God has shown us, and, in light of this historical prologue, let us love him and keep his commandments. May we throw away all idols, including the idol of self-centeredness, and confess exclusive loyalty to the Sovereign Lord.

If we are parents, may we serve the Lord wholeheartedly and so bring untold blessings to our children and their children for generations to come. May we carefully study the covenant document, the Bible, to do what it commands and avoid what it forbids. May we govern our families for the Lord and warn them as watchmen, always remembering that we must give an account to the Lord for those who are under our charge. Let us emulate Joshua and renew our covenant to serve the Lord both now and forevermore.

CONCLUSION

Victory in Jesus! This fact must stir our hearts to rejoice and give thanks to the triune God. Christians too often misunderstand the meaning of Christ's triumph and ignore its mandate for our lives. Today, any mention of salvation through Jesus Christ alone is considered narrow-minded and intolerant. Many Christians glibly believe that, having made a profession of faith, they can claim God's blessings regardless of obedience. Others ignore altogether the fact that as Christians they are called to live in covenant relationship with other believers in a local church. The book of Joshua corrects such errors.

Victory is in Jesus precisely because he is the victor. We have seen how the Lord is a warrior who will conquer every enemy who obstinately refuses to surrender. This awesome God never changes—Jesus must and will punish every sin and every unrepentant sinner. Every Canaanite king loses, both here and hereafter.

Victory is in Jesus, but it is shared only by those who, like Rahab, believe on him. Those who fled to a city of refuge found mercy in Joshua's day; likewise, we must flee to Jesus Christ, the true city of refuge, to receive everlasting salvation from God's just wrath against sin. Everyone who calls on the name of the Lord will be saved.

Victory is in Jesus, and God's people today have battles to fight, just like Joshua of old. Our enemies are not flesh and blood, but spiritual enemies, including sin and Satan, who daily tempt and try to deceive us. This warfare will continue until Christ's climactic return. We must know and obey God's word, seek his will in every situation, and exhort and help one another. We can take great encouragement in the fact that we will win because our triune God wins!

Victory in Jesus! Are you discouraged, depressed, or defeated? Surrender fully to Jesus Christ. Repudiate your sin, ask God to forgive you for Jesus' sake, and place your trust in Christ alone. Become a vital member of a Bible-believing church and begin to live a life of fidelity to the Bible—the covenant document that governs faith and conduct. God guarantees success in this life and the life to come for all who, like Joshua, follow him wholeheartedly. Then you too will discover that "not one of all the good promises the Lord your God gave you has failed" (Josh. 23:14).

Bibliography

Boice, James Montgomery. *Joshua: We Will Serve the Lord.* Old Tappan, NJ: Fleming H. Revell Co., 1989.

Henry, Matthew. *Complete Commentary on the Whole Bible,* vol. 2. Old Tappan, NJ: Fleming H. Revell Co., n.d.

Hess, Richard S. *Joshua: An Introduction and Commentary.* Downers Grove, IL: InterVarsity Press, 1996.

Lloyd-Jones, D. Martyn. *Life in Two Kingdoms: An Exposition of Romans 13.* Edinburgh: Banner of Truth Trust, 2000.

Madvig, Donald H. *Joshua.* Vol. 3 of *Expositor's Bible Commentary: Deuteronomy–2 Samuel,* edited by Frank E. Gaebelein, et al. Grand Rapids, MI: Zondervan, 1981.

Pink, Arthur W. *Gleanings in Joshua.* Chicago: Moody Press, 1964.

Rushdoony, R. J. *Institutes of Biblical Law.* Nutley, NJ: Craig Press, 1977.

Schaeffer, Francis A. *Escape from Reason.* Downers Grove, IL: InterVarsity Press, 1968.

Schaeffer, Francis A. *Joshua and the Flow of Biblical History.* Downers Grove, IL: InterVarsity Press, 1976.

Stott, John. *Guard the Truth: The Message of 1 Timothy and Titus.* Downers Grove, IL: InterVarsity Press, 1996.

Woudstra, Marten H. *New International Commentary on the Old Testament: The Book of Joshua.* Grand Rapids, MI: Eerdmans, 1981.

Subject Index

A

Abraham. *See* covenant with
Achan 65–71, 84–85, 129
Ai 68–70, 84
allotment of land 110, 112,
    126, 127
altar of sacrifice 75, 77, 81
angels 52, 87, 98, 104, 105
angel of the Lord 50–51
ark of covenant 42–43, 47,
    61, 79
atonement. *See* Day of
    Atonement; forgiveness
autonomy 6, 15, 22, 55–56, 69
avenger of blood 117, 119–120

B

Balaam 50, 148
belief 3, 11–12, 28, 38–42, 61,
    90, 111. *See also* faith
Bible. *See* word of God
blessings. *See* obedience: bless-
    ings for

C

Caleb 38, 109–116, 127
Canaan
    conquest of 21, 85–86,
        97–103, 114

promised 3, 4, 26, 39, 41,
    112. *See also* promises of
    God: land
Canaanites
    fear of 26, 28, 39, 57
    sin of 26, 50, 52–53, 62, 85,
        99, 103
capital punishment 118–119
captain of the Lord's army
    49–53, 56, 58, 64, 148
cities of refuge 117–124
confession 28–29, 67, 70, 71,
    80
confidence 40, 56–57, 111
consecration 40, 44, 69–70
constitutional convention
    73–82
covenant. *See also* promises
    of God
    and family 155–156
    prohibited 85–86
    renewal 18–20, 146
    sanctions 153–154
    stipulations 149–152
    with Abraham 3, 4, 38, 75,
        148
    with church 65–66, 71, 81,
        129
    with Israel 74–75, 137,
        145–157

covenant-keeping 15–24
curse 50, 76, 78, 102, 106.
    See also disobedience:
    curses for

D

Day of Atonement 47
death penalty. See capital pun-
    ishment
deception 31–32, 68, 86–93
decision-making 17–18, 24,
    83–95, 154–155
defeat
    of enemies by God 10–11,
        58, 103, 148–149
    result of sin 68–69, 84–85
demons 63, 87, 147–148, 151
disobedience
    curses for 23, 76–82, 129,
        142, 153

E

Ebal 73–82

F

faith
    and victory 55–64, 114–115
    aspects of 109–115
    steps of 27–30
    works of 30–34, 113–114,
        151
faithfulness of God 40, 135–
    144. See also promises
    of God
false prophets 90, 91
fear
    of enemies 38, 58, 101, 113.
        See also Canaanites:
        fear of
    of God 12, 106, 149–150

fighting
    God fights for us 11, 58, 103,
        111, 138, 141–142
    we must fight 3, 13, 56, 107,
        113, 115, 159–160
forgiveness 47, 70, 71, 81, 121,
    143

G

Gerizim 73–82
giants 10, 109, 111, 113,
    114–115
Gibeonites 16, 85–88, 93,
    100–101
giving. See tithing
God's will 2, 16, 115
gospel
    declared 9, 27, 45, 46, 64,
        106, 111, 122
    false 90, 151
grace of God 27, 34, 77, 149
guarantee. See covenant;
    promises of God
guidance 39, 42, 89, 90

H

hanged 101–106
Hebron 102, 109–116, 127
hell 33, 47, 82, 123
holiness
    of God 11, 53, 69, 147
    required of us 12, 35, 40,
        107, 139
Holy Spirit 29, 34, 107, 114,
    150

I

idols
    money 18, 24, 66, 152
    pagan 62–63, 80, 139–140,
        147–148, 152–154

self 15–16, 23, 152, 157
inheritance 13, 21, 82, 115–116, 126, 138
inquiring of God 83–95

J

Jacob's well 75, 80
Jericho 26–27, 50, 57
Jesus Christ
  greater Joshua 13, 47–48, 79–80, 90–93, 143–144
  Judge 50, 51, 63, 82, 99, 105, 124
  Lord 53, 151
  refuge 120–124
  sacrifice 16, 47–48, 78, 106
  Savior 35, 63–64, 80, 120–124
  Warrior 13, 50–51, 104
Jordan River
  crossing 10, 20, 37–44
judge. *See* Jesus Christ: Judge
judgment
  final 98, 105, 124
  of Canaanites 62, 99, 103
  of sinners 51, 67, 99, 123

K

kindness of God 62–64, 99, 108

L

law of God 75–79, 106, 128.
  See also word of God
Levites 125–128
love
  for God 22, 30, 113, 116, 140–141, 152
  for others 24
  of God 25, 35, 141, 149, 157

M

meditate 7–8
memorial 44–47
ministerial support 130–132
murder 117–119

N

Noah's ark 124

O

obedience
  and victory 59–62. *See also* faith: and victory
  blessings for 6–7, 19, 22–23, 76–82, 129, 142, 153
  commanded 6–7, 20–22, 53, 59–62, 139, 141
  evidence of faith 30–31, 113–114, 116

P

patience 61, 109–110, 114–115
prayer 29–30, 33, 83–95, 112
presence of God 9–12, 39, 42–43, 53, 69, 79, 102
problems solved 43–44, 47–48, 58–59
promises of God
  claimed 111–112
  fulfilled 12–13, 138–139
  his presence 9–12, 39, 79
  land 3–5, 38–40, 111–112
  salvation 29–30, 33–34, 42
  success 1, 3–5, 40–42, 56–57
promises of man 16, 18–22, 65

R

Rahab 25–36, 63
reductionism 52, 68, 99
regeneration 29–30, 114

repentance 18–20, 67, 70, 80, 99, 106, 107
rest 10, 13–19, 116, 122, 137, 138, 143

S

sacrifice 77–79
salvation
  and works 30–31
  in Christ 13, 35–36, 46, 80, 99, 106, 120–122, 143–144, 149, 159. *See also* Jesus Christ: Savior
  of families 8–9, 32–34, 145–146, 155–156
  of Rahab 25, 63
  steps of 27–30, 81
Satan 87–88, 90, 141, 147, 160
Saul of Tarsus 53
Scripture. *See* word of God
Second Coming 82, 98, 107
self-righteousness 25, 77, 78, 80
self-will 84, 152
selfishness 15–18, 23
servant 1, 52, 114, 118, 136, 151
severity of God. *See* wrath of God
Shechem 74–75, 79–81, 145
sin
  causes of 11, 68, 150
  in church 17–18, 66–70, 151
  of Canaanites. *See* Canaanites: sin of
  remedy for 8, 69–70, 107, 114, 121
  results of 23, 68–69, 153

sinners 25, 27, 47, 71, 78, 120–121, 124, 143, 149
spies 10, 26, 28, 31–32, 38–39, 84, 110
stealing 66–67, 128–129
stewardship 125–134
success
  guaranteed 3–5, 160
  how to achieve 5–9, 12–13, 90–95, 113, 136–137
surrender
  necessary for salvation 52, 53, 64, 106, 159–160
suzerainty treaty 146–154
sword 50–51, 63, 118–122

T

tithing 125–134
two and a half tribes 17–22

U

unbelief 28, 38–39, 42, 111, 115, 140

V

victory
  faith and 55–64, 114–115
  in battle 21, 60, 104, 114–115
  in Christ 47–48, 56–58, 159
  over sin 56–58

W

warrior 11, 50, 103, 159. *See also* Jesus Christ: Savior
will of God 2, 5, 16, 53, 84, 85, 89–90, 93, 112, 115, 150, 155

word of God 5–9, 41, 46–47,
59–61, 73, 76–77, 81,
89, 111, 139, 151, 153
works. *See* faith: works of
worship
of God 12, 52, 115, 132

of idols 139–140, 152. *See
also* idols
wrath of God 47, 51, 63–64,
77, 99, 104, 122, 124

Grace and Glory Ministries

GRACE & GLORY
MINISTRIES

Grace and Glory Ministries is an extension of Grace Valley Christian Center. We are committed to the teaching of God's infallible word. It is our mission to proclaim the whole gospel to the whole world for the building up of the whole body of Christ.

For more information on the ministries of Grace Valley Christian Center, please visit:

http://www.gracevalley.org

To obtain additional copies of this book, please e-mail:

gvcc@gracevalley.org

ALSO FROM GRACE & GLORY MINISTRIES

The Normal Church Life
An Exposition of the First Epistle of John
P. G. Mathew

Paperback, 304 pages

"I am delighted to strongly recommend Pastor Mathew's recent book. I have been blessed for several years by listening to Pastor Mathew's sermons on tape. The printed word nicely captures the clarity, wisdom, and power of the actual sermons."

—Dr. Henry F. Schaefer III, Professor of Chemistry,
University of Georgia, and author of
Science and Christianity: Conflict or Coherence?

"Few things will bless you more than a careful reading of the First Epistle of John. This masterful exposition of that epistle by P. G. Mathew will make that blessing palpable."

—Dr. William A. Dembski, Research Professor in Philosophy,
Southwestern Baptist Theological Seminary (Ft. Worth),
and author of *The Design Inference.*

"The church of our Lord Jesus Christ is not merely a social institution. Rather, it is an entirely divine institution . . . one in which love rules all thoughts and actions. But each Christian loves his brother or sister in Christ only because of his faith—his relationship with the Christ of Scripture. Such faith produces new life, new love, and new obedience. This love is 'the normal church life.' Oh, how we need more of that normalcy in the church of our day!"

—Alan R. Moak, Pastor and Editor

For ordering information, please contact:

GRACE & GLORY MINISTRIES
gvcc@gracevalley.org
http://www.gracevalley.org